T0358234

Business, Government and Sustainable Development

Today sustainability thinking encompasses a wide range of national and international ecological concerns, socio-economic issues and topics on democratic institutional development. The involved policy processes demand the engagement of an equally diverse group of actors. This book analyses a new stage emerging in the development of sustainability policies from the Netherlands and shows how this phase poses new strategic questions to business and governments.

The author highlights the increasing complexity of the changing process towards sustainable development and illustrates the importance of collaboration between businesses, governments and non-governmental organisations in the design and implementation of shared strategies for sustainable development.

The book then moves to questions of business administration related to the strategic management of the shift to sustainable business. It demonstrates how businesses can arrange internal and external organisational processes for the development of strategies to utilise the potential of sustainable development. It illustrates the importance of stakeholder collaboration for better achievement of sustainable business objectives.

This book shows sustainable business to be an inspiring, innovative and rewarding aspect of entrepreneurship and will be essential reading for students and researchers of sustainable development, environmental management and the evolution of environmental policy.

Gerard Keijzers is Professor of Sustainable Entrepreneurship at Nyenrode University, The Netherlands Business School. He gained practical experience in this field of work during the 1990s when he was Director for Strategy in the Dutch Ministry of Environment and a member of the OECD group on environmental performance in Paris, France.

Routledge Advances in Management and Business Studies

Business, Government and Sustainable Development

Gerard Keijzers

Routledge
Taylor & Francis Group

LONDON AND NEW YORK

First published 2005
by Routledge
2 Park Square, Milton Park, Abingdon, Oxon OX14 4RN

Simultaneously published in the USA and Canada
by Routledge
270 Madison Avenue, New York, NY 10016

Routledge is an imprint of the Taylor & Francis Group

© 2005 Gerard Keijzers

Typeset in Sabon by
HWA Text and Data Management, Tunbridge Wells

British Library Cataloguing in Publication Data
A catalogue record for this book is available from the British Library

Library of Congress Cataloging in Publication Data
Keijzers, Gerard.
  Business, government, and sustainable development /
  Gerard Keijzers.
     p.   cm.
  Includes bibliographical references and index.
1. Sustainable development–Netherlands. 2. Netherlands–Economic
policy. I. Title.
  HC329.5.E5K45 2004
  338.9492'07–dc22   2004001854

ISBN 0–415–33963–4

Contents

Preface

A few years ago, when I still was the director for Strategy in the Netherlands' Ministry of the Environment (Ministry of VROM), I was granted the opportunity for a two-month sabbatical at MIT in Boston, USA. I intended to write a paper to document an analysis of the Dutch environmental policy experience that would serve as a guide for policy makers in other countries. The Netherlands' environmental policy had proven quite successful and become well known internationally. As such, the Netherlands' environmental policy was seen as an interesting empirical example of advanced environmental policy development. The Dutch collaborative approach of 'covenants' with industry and local governments, the Netherlands' environmental tax policies, and its codification of environmental regulation into a comprehensive Environmental Act, presented attractive examples of a successful environmental policy 'experiment' in a country of 16 million people.

With the guidance and inspiring support of Prof. dr. L. Susskind, Ford Professor of Urban and Environmental Planning at MIT and Director of the Negotiation Program at Harvard Law School, I set out making my analyses. At that time, I could not expect that this article would mark the beginning of a series of articles that would lead to the book at hand. Neither did I expect that this would become a start of a scientific career when I was given the opportunity to accept the position of professor of Sustainable Entrepreneurship at Nyenrode University in the Netherlands. Throughout this process Prof. dr. W. Hafkamp, the Dean of the Faculty of Social Sciences of the Erasmus University of Rotterdam, has been an important counselor and a dear friend.

I thank my colleague Ronald Jeurissen, professor of Business Ethics at Nyenrode University, with whom I developed an inspiring research relationship and started at Nyenrode University, the Center for Sustainability. We conduct research and advisory services on issues related to managing sustainability and ethics in businesses. I thank Ronald Jeurissen for co-authoring Chapter 3 of this book.

I also wish to express my gratitude to dr. Frank Boons of the Erasmus University in Rotterdam who co-authored Chapter 5 of this book.

I especially wish to thank Ms Mei Li Han (MBA) for editing this book and performing all the thousands of tasks involved in completing the manuscript.

I respectfully acknowledge the willingness of several publishers to allow me to use for this book the (edited and expanded versions of) original articles that appeared in their international scientific journals before, including Elsevier Publishers, The Society for Business Ethics, and Greenleaf Publishing Limited.

I want to take this opportunity to thank the Ministry of VROM and The Social Venture Network in The Netherlands, the sponsors of the Chair of Sustainable Entrepreneurship at Nyenrode University, which I hold at present.

The Netherlands' Ministry of VROM (Environmental Protection) continued to support my research efforts.

The Social Venture Network is an inspiring group of over a hundred Dutch companies, which aim to establish new responsible and sustainable ways of doing business. It is part of a worldwide network that carries the same name. Social and environmental responsibility is the fundamental business principle of these enterprises. I have come to learn them well by now, and I found that the group of people united in this association, definitely is a group of responsible people, but above all they bring inspiration, innovation and 'fun'.

I think that the words: responsibility, inspiration, innovation, creativity, and fun express the real meaning of sustainable entrepreneurship. Certainly we owe a debt to others in less fortunate conditions elsewhere in the world, and surely we owe it to the generations after us. We are indeed responsible for the living conditions of others now and in the future. But taking on this responsibility will be the most productive if we can do the work in inspiring, creative and pleasant ways. Then responsibility of creating new ways of doing business is not a burden but a delight and an honor.

And, that is exactly what I attempt to teach my students. Sustainable business is business that is rewarding in economic, social and ecological terms. Without these rewards sustainable business would not exist. Inspiring and innovative people create these new ways of doing business. Not because they must, but because they want to experience the desire and the delight of sustainable entrepreneurship.

Gerard Keijzers
January 2004
The Hague, The Netherlands

Acknowledgements

I respectfully acknowledge the willingness of several publishers to allow me to use and reprint (revised and expanded versions) of articles that appeared in their international scientific journals before:

Elsevier Publishers

An early version of Chapter 2 was published as 'Evolution of Dutch environmental policy from 1970–2000, and beyond: the changing ecological arena', (2000) in the *Journal of Cleaner Production*, 8: 179–200.

An abridged version of Chapter 4 of this book was published as 'The transition to the sustainable enterprise', (2002) in the *Journal of Cleaner Production*, 10: 349–59.

Society for Business Ethics

An abbreviated version of Chapter 3 was published as 'Future generations and business ethics', (2004) in the *Business Ethics Quarterly*, 14, 1: 47–69.

Greenleaf Publishing Limited

An earlier version of Chapter 6 was published as 'Creating sustainable directions: evolving stakeholder approaches in seven multinationals', (2003) in the *Journal of Corporate Citizenship*, 10, Summer: 79–88.

Abbreviations

CFCs	chlorofluorocarbons
CO_2	carbon dioxide
CR	corporate responsibility
MIT	Massachusetts Institute of Technology
mpl	milligrams per litre
NEPP	National Environmental Policy Plan
NGOs	non-governmental organisations
NO_x	nitrogen oxide
OECD	Organisation for Economic Co-operation and Development
RIVM	National Research Institute for Public Health and the Environment (the Netherlands)
SMEs	small and medium enterprises
SO_2	sulphur dioxide
UN	United Nations
UNCED	United Nations Conference on Environment and Development
VROM	Ministry of Housing, Spacial Planning and Environmental Protection (the Netherlands)
WBCSD	World Business Council for Sustainable Development
WCED	World Commission on Environment and Development
WSSD	World Summit on Sustainable Development

1 Introduction

Over time, the range of sustainability objectives has developed from relatively simple issues of environmental protection to encompass international and national social, economic and ecological issues. A closer examination of the evolving range of sustainability issues, and the involved changes within governments and businesses, reveals a complex process. Related to this complexity are the benefits of a collaborative stakeholder approach in achieving objectives of sustainable development. The aim of this study is investigating these change processes in the public and the private sector and analysing the potential benefits of a collaborative stakeholder approach.

Governments continue to fine-tune policies for the sustainable development of society, while the business community strives towards enhanced corporate ecological and social responsibility. This requires understanding a government-based perspective and subsequently concentrating on the business perspective of developing and implementing strategies for the sustainability of enterprises.

To understand the evolving conditions for governments and businesses, a concise historical review of the development of the changing arenas of sustainability is provided first as a basis for consideration.

The changing ecological arena

In August 2002, exactly 30 years after the first United Nations (UN) conference on these issues in Stockholm, Sweden, and 10 years after the second conference in Rio de Janeiro, Brazil, the United Nations' World Summit on Sustainable Development (WSSD) was held in Johannesburg, South Africa. While understanding and acting on the outcomes of the Johannesburg conference is a long-term endeavour, both earlier events set in motion important policy processes for improving sustainable development in the world. The nations, businesses and people that gathered in Johannesburg again pledged to continue and intensify the realisation of actions for sustainable development (WSSD 2002).

From a historical perspective, this process began at the conference in Stockholm in 1972, when full political attention for issues related to environmental protection and safeguarding conditions of health and safety for people and ecosystems gained attention for the first time. In the wake of this conference, a political movement was awakened, leading to a body of environmental legislation in many countries around the world. Basic principles of environmental protection slowly entered legislation and the thinking of people and businesses. The policy principle of, for instance, 'the polluter pays' was born in Stockholm and slowly grew to maturity in national and international regulations, despite its immediate acceptance and proliferation by the Organisation for Economic Co-operation and Development (OECD) countries. In parallel, the 'precautionary principle' adopted in the Rio de Janeiro conference in 1992 continues to develop and awaits adoption in government regulations and business practices. Gradually these policy processes have resulted in a remarkable improvement in environmental conditions since the beginning of the work in 1972.

During the course of the 1980s the attention given to environmental quality protection issues widened to include ecological issues related to the preservation of resource stocks (energy, water, biodiversity, minerals). These quantitative aspects of ecological control (in addition to the qualitative aspects of environmental protection of air, water and soil) were identified earlier as important issues by the Club of Rome, in 1972. Nonetheless, these issues only received full political recognition with the international acceptance of the *Brundtland Report* in 1987 (World Commission on Environment and Development [WCED] 1987). This report links the social, economic and ecological interests of present and future generations, including the range of relatively simple environmental protection issues and sustainability issues.

Within the *Brundtland Report*, sustainability is defined as a development in which present generations satisfy their own needs without compromising the ability of future generations to satisfy their needs. The challenge in this definition lies in the implicit double responsibility. In one instance, the moral duty to address today's world poverty and inequality is determined, and at the same time the responsibility to ensure adequate production opportunities for future generations through the preservation of available natural capital is expressed. Thus, sustainable development is linked to the realisation of lasting economic growth, equitable distribution of economic welfare amongst present generations, equitable distribution of natural capital between generations, adjusting consumption patterns, limiting population growth rates and innovating production technologies to maintain production growth within the planet's ecological absorption capacity.

This challenging task shared by all actors in society was included in *Agenda 21*, established at the United Nations Conference on Environment and Development in Rio de Janeiro (UNCED 1992), and included in the Conventions on Biodiversity and Climate Change. Ten years later, it is possible to observe the important policy developments related to these issues of sustainability. The Biodiversity Convention has been implemented in national legislation on nature protection in many countries. Similarly, important developments on the reduction of CO_2 emissions have taken place since the Rio Climate Convention of 1992 and the Kyoto Protocol of 1997. The US withdrawal from the latter agreement is, for the time being, a significant setback in achieving the objectives formulated in the Protocol. However, at the recent Johannesburg summit the minimum requirement of 55 ratifying countries – together accountable for at least 55 per cent of the world's total CO_2 emission – was nearly met, increasing the power of the Kyoto Protocol as an effective and binding piece of international legislation for all ratifying countries.

Taken together these documents and reports are a sign of progress towards declared objectives of sustainable development. And related actions such as *Agenda 21* can be seen as drivers of a determined, ongoing and increasingly complex process of change that engages an ever-growing number of people, businesses and nations.

The Johannesburg Declaration determines the major challenges of sustainable development as follows:

- We recognize that poverty eradication, changing consumption and production patterns, and protecting the natural resource base for economic and social development are overarching objectives of, and essential requirements for, sustainable development.
- The deep fault line that divides human society between the rich and the poor and the ever-increasing gap between the developed and developing worlds, pose a major threat to global prosperity, security and stability.
- The global environment continues to suffer. Loss of biodiversity continues, fish stocks continue to be depleted, desertification claims more and more fertile land, the adverse effects of climate change are already evident, natural disasters are more frequent and more devastating and developing countries more vulnerable, and air,

water and marine pollution continue to rob millions of a decent life.

(WSSD 2002: 2)

Today sustainability thinking encompasses socioeconomic issues, topics on democratic institutional development and international security, and a wide range of ecological concerns. And the involved policy processes demand the engagement of an equally diverse group of actors in governments and business.

Addressing both the evolving substance matter and the changing collaborative societal processes of sustainable development is central to this study. An examination of strategic change processes both from government and business perspectives allows an analysis of the evolution of government policies that are developing from a traditional and regulatory 'command and control' approach to a voluntary and collaborative approach of consensus-building with the private sector. And further, the research extends to the broad societal processes of 'transition' to new socio-technological systems for sustainable development. Thus, there is an increasing preparedness and need in the private sector to engage in a stakeholder approach to jointly design and implement business strategies for sustainable production processes and products.

The aim and structure of the research

In nearly all scenarios, policies and strategies for sustainable development relate to decision-making processes to resolve competing socio-economic and ecological objectives that involve stakeholder interests. This study therefore highlights the increasing complexity of the change process towards sustainable development, and the necessity to intensify the collaboration between the parties involved to ensure committed and enduring change. And the study illustrates the importance of collaboration between governments, businesses and non-governmental organisations in the design and implementation of government and business strategies and practices for sustainable development.

The two main research questions of this study are formulated:

1   How does the complex and broadening range of sustainability issues affect policy processes of governments and businesses?

First, the evolving sustainability agenda for governments and businesses, and the consequences of engaging stakeholders in related policy processes, are analysed. Subsequently, the research focuses on questions considering whether present generations actually bear ethical responsibilities for future generations to achieve a sustainable development, and how businesses can deal with the consequences of these responsibilities. Then, the operational questions of how the new issues of sustainability can affect enterprises and how governments and businesses can jointly contribute to achieve the conditions that allow for a shift to the sustainable enterprise are examined.

2 How can enterprises manage the strategic processes of adapting their resources and capabilities to the new demands for sustainability from a growing number of stakeholders?

The research questions posed in the first part of this study symbolise the increasingly complex policy process that requires intensified stakeholder engagement in the development of business strategies for sustainable development. In turn, this leads to business administration research questions related to the strategic management of the shift to sustainable business. The way businesses can arrange internal and external processes for the development of strategies to utilise the potential of sustainable development is analysed. And the question of why and how intensified processes of stakeholder collaboration can be structured for better achievement of sustainable business objectives is addressed.

This research integrates the important theoretical perspectives of the 'consensus-building theory' (Susskind 1999), the 'stakeholder theory' (Freeman 1984), and the strategic management theory of 'resource-based views' (Kay 1996). These theories all show the importance of transparency and flexibility in processes of collaboration and joint learning to achieve committed changes and allow for adequate treatment of all interests at stake.

Beginning with an investigation into the development of the evolving issues and processes related to policies of environmental protection, the discussion moves toward policies for sustainable development. Policy development in the Netherlands provides an example for further consideration.

A historical analysis of the development of Dutch environmental policies from 1970 to 2000 covers all relevant policy documents of the various Dutch Ministries, as well as related important literature describing and analysing the development of these policies in the Netherlands.[1] A series of interviews with staff of the Dutch Environment Ministry supports the analysis. The environmental problems addressed by the government have grown increasingly complex due to shifts in the content focus and the extending range of environmental issues. In addition, the nature of policy processes changed as a result of the growing number of involved parties, and the increased intensity of related cross-sectoral interests. It is shown that environmental problems developed from rather singular technical issues of environmental protection related to complex issues of resource stock management. Increasingly these preservation strategies connect to cross-sectoral socio-economic and environmental interests, requiring complex processes of stakeholder engagement and consensus-building.

The future agenda for achieving sustainability, shows the complex ecological and social-economic issues calling for fundamental 'transitions' in technology and technological production and consumption systems, and in the related institutional, cultural and socioeconomic settings. Adopting an integrated approach to engage all relevant social, economic and ecological stakeholders in order to effectively create new directions for sustainability is key. This is evidenced by whole supply chains, new technology chains, surroundings of businesses – nationally and internationally – and interests of future generations that are included in the approach.

Historical analysis demonstrates the relevance and topicality of present policy developments with respect to dilemmas regarding inter- and intra-generational responsibilities for use of natural capital resources, as formulated by the Brundtland Commission. Present management of natural capital resources casts a shadow far into the future. Consumption rates of non-renewable energy resources and the degradation of biodiversity affect life conditions of future generations, posing fundamental ethical questions on the responsibility for future generations.

Ethical theory leads to the conclusion that present generations have substantial responsibilities for future generations in preserving ecological conditions. At the same time, it shows the complexity of transposing these responsibilities into concrete policy objectives for sustainability. Research shows that due to differences in risk and moral perception, there are no unique solutions to questions of intergenerational distribution. Subsequently, it is argued that all societal parties intensively engage in a societal process to collaboratively design and interactively build the societal road to sustainable development in which present generations satisfy present needs without compromising the ability of future generations to satisfy their needs.

The findings of a related literature search are tested in two practical case studies. The first case study reviews the preservation strategies for the limited natural gas reserves in the Netherlands and the implications for intergenerational responsibility. The second case study discusses the protection of biodiversity stocks in relation to the development of a new road in the south of the Netherlands.

On the grounds of a variety of ethical and socio-psychological reasons it is concluded that responsibility for future generations, who have the same rights and entitlements as present generations, and to whom present generations want to extend justice, must be taken. More specifically, the intergenerational responsibility of companies dealing with complicated problems raise the following questions:

- What is the specific responsibility of business for the preservation of scarce mineral resources and for investing in a timely transition to durable energy sources?
- How do companies assess and control their impact on biodiversity?
- What views might business leaders adopt in the debate on technological potential and the risks of transition towards more sustainable production processes and products?

Companies share in the common responsibility to future generations. Companies can learn to deal with questions of scientific uncertainty and potential risks for future generations. Participatory ethics that shape the corporate, social and ecological responsibilities towards present and future generations can be realised by processes of stakeholder engagement. Participatory ethics specifically relates to a revaluation of civil society to engage in the fulfillment of future-oriented responsibilities. And there is a call for a 'third arena', in addition to the 'first' (political institutions) and 'second arena' (the market), to enable permanent discussions between business and society on issues of sustainability. The importance of the 'precautionary principle' as an essential tool to guide these processes of stakeholder collaboration and consensus-building is central.

The discussion around intergenerational responsibilities of companies leads to questions of why and how companies can make the transition to become sustainable enterprises. The agenda of new sustainability issues facing the business community focuses on elements that are woven around related social and ecological issues of resource stock management and of technology development for sustainable energy production, land use and biodiversity preservation.

This indicates that the 'license to operate' is not a static concept, but a dynamic entity, requiring continuous maintenance at two levels. First, the daily management of the company demands continuous adjustments to meet the changing sustainability demands with which the company is confronted. Second, there is a need for companies to continuously and collaboratively work with other companies and governments on the improvement of social, economic, technological and infrastructural production conditions of the company. Sustainable business requires production conditions determined by the quality of the infrastructure for energy supply and transportation, the institutional qualities of society, and the level and focus of the work force. A next step is developing a program for businesses and governments to create the necessary conditions to allow transition to sustainable entrepreneurship for the business community as a whole, guiding individual businesses in making the change to become a sustainable enterprise.

Establishing a need for enterprises to make a transition to become sustainable calls for management strategies to realise such changes. Applying modern business administration views on 'stakeholder theory' (e.g. stakeholder engagement, organisational learning and action–learning networks) and 'resource-based theory' (the strategic management of a company's distinctive resources and capabilities) to the development of a systematic management perspective on sustainable business is explored. This perspective concerns both the internal management of strategic change and the external management of the company's relationship with its stakeholders. In an empirical investigation, the advancement of strategies for sustainable business in 11 multinationals in the Netherlands was tested. The research was guided by two questions:

1 Are companies entering a new management stage in which new sustainability issues dominate the agenda involving a wider array of stakeholders?
2 How are companies managing the strategic process of adapting their internal resources to these new demands of this enlarging number of stakeholders?

To support the analysis, a series of analytic elements were developed to test the advancement of business strategy development (e.g. regarding organisational routines). To further support the empirical analysis, a stage-model was developed to analyse the advancement of companies toward sustainability in three stages.

The research leads to lessons on the need to intensively collaborate with company stakeholders to achieve joint learning processes and to realise a committed transition to sustainable ways of production. And recommendations to companies to establish the next stage of sustainable entrepreneurship with respect to the internal organisational adjustment processes and the external change processes in collaboration with stakeholders are presented.

The research further focuses on the importance of a collaborative stakeholder approach for business strategies relating to corporate social and ecological responsibility (CR) and possible ways to intensify processes to engage the company's stakeholders. An empirical study on the evolution of stakeholder approaches for CR strategies focused on the practices in seven multinational corporations in the United Kingdom and the Netherlands. The research questions guiding this investigation were: why is it important for companies to engage with stakeholders to learn about CR issues, and how can companies integrate this stakeholder approach into their organisational structures?

The research examines the differences between long-term value drivers for CR business strategies (to enhance the company's continuity) and short-term value drivers (for reputation management). From this empirical and theoretical research, a number of recommendations on stakeholder approaches for the development of CR business policies that underline the assumed benefits of intensive and collaborative stakeholder approach are presented.

In the concluding chapter of this work, the societal advantages and business benefits of a collaborative stakeholder approach and of consensus-building policies of governments and enterprises are reviewed. Also the importance of joint learning and discovery processes to address differing risk attitudes and differing risk perceptions about the development and introduction of new technologies is discussed. This summary ends with conclusions and suggestions to enterprises on operationalising and intensification of the collaborative stakeholder processes.

2 The changing ecological arena

In the past 30 years, environmental policy in the Netherlands has evolved through three distinct phases. From 1970 to 1983, delimiting the ecological policy arena was the aim. Efforts during this phase focused on cleaning up pollution after it occurred. In the second phase, from 1984 to 1989, the aim was ensuring pollution prevention. The third phase, from 1990 to the present, has emphasised eco-efficiency and encouraged the integration of ecological and economic concerns. It appears that a fourth phase is about to begin, with a broader international scope and highlighted by a multisectoral concern for sustainability (see Table 2.1).

This evolution has influenced the instruments of policy implementation, with the transition from one phase to the next marked by new experience and understanding. A survey of the forces propelling the evolution of Dutch environmental policy crystallises the most important lessons for those shaping the next generation of environmental policies in the Netherlands and elsewhere. And special attention is given to the role of technology and technological change in this process.

Three phases in the evolution of Dutch environmental policy

Until the late 1960s, the Nuisance Act of 1875 was the only legislation authorising municipal governments to abate serious pollution at the local level, and this law was rather limited. With the passage of the Pollution of Surface Water Act in 1969 and the Air Pollution Act in 1970, the first steps were taken to define the 'ecological arena' (i.e. the full slate of environmental issues) as an area of national concern in and of itself. Indeed, these laws marked the beginning of a decade where comprehensive legislation was created to manage numerous aspects of the natural environment (De Koning 1994: 204).[1] The 1972 publication

Table 2.1 Evolution of environmental policies in the Netherlands, 1970–2000

Period and classification	Focus of environmental policies	Style of decision making	Instruments
Phase 1: 1970–83 *Shaping the ecological arena* Improving national conditions for human health	Clean up air and water pollution; begin soil clean-up operations	Top–down formulation of national legislation and definition of quality standards; no stakeholder involvement	National and European legislation; regulatory licensing enforced by local authorities; add-on technology
Phase 2: 1984–9 *Encouraging pollution prevention* Protecting national health conditions for humans and ecosystems	Prevent pollution in order to preserve air, water, soil and biodiversity; begin to focus on acidification and ozone depletion	Some stakeholder involvement in design and implementation of programs; allowing room for technology choices and flexible timing	Emission reduction targets; environmental care; environmental impact assessment; financial incentives; legal liability; stricter enforcement
Phase 3: 1990–9 *Enhancing eco-efficiency* In addition to previous actions, taking on international responsibility for global air quality	Increase attention on the transnational issues of acidification, global warming, and ozone depletion	Granting of greater autonomy to local authorities and private enterprise to set objectives; more flexible design and implementation	Targets, target groups; covenants; economic, technological, fiscal and social instruments; general rules for small and medium enterprises
Phase 4: 2000–present *Super-optimisation for sustainable development* Opportunities for multi-sectoral benefits	Increase attention on limiting usage and improving management of global stocks of biodiversity, energy and minerals	Integration of ecological, economic and social interests, nationally and internationally; new processes to develop joint objectives	Target global resources; incentives for producers, consumers; new forums; breakthrough technologies; get prices right; quality consumption

of the *Policy Document on the Urgency of Environmental Pollution* by the newly established Environmental Protection Department greatly enhanced both the implementation of environmental policies and the profile of environmental issues in the public eye (VROM 1972).

The search for new and more effective environmental policies grew out of public concern over serious air and water pollution and soil contamination in industrial and densely populated areas. The focus at this time was on restoring conditions conducive to public health and achieving a set of ambitious objectives within 10 years. These objectives included cleaning up pollution from the past and remediating damage, reducing the accumulation of solid wastes, limiting noise, radiation and thermal pollution, and reducing the deposition of chemical waste and exhaust fumes.

The action program included in the *Policy Document on the Urgency of Environmental Pollution* targeted agriculture, industry and transportation as the major polluters. Most of the 63 actions spelled out in the report involved the development of specific legislation to clean up air, water, soil, waste and noise pollution. The program called for the imposition of strict emission standards on production processes, as well as new permitting procedures to be enforced by municipal authorities.

The legislation and the tools for its implementation were formulated at the national level, with little or no involvement of stakeholders or the local authorities responsible for enforcing the new permitting systems. The environmental quality standards specified in the legislation set new limits on the economic and social activities of private enterprises, consumers and local authorities. The top-down legislative approach chosen by the Environmental Protection Department was viewed as the only way to establish the boundaries and the importance of the ecological arena as an entity of its own. The approach was justified by the threats to public health that would result from the continued degradation of the natural environment.

The new laws and the policies rested on a number of general principles adopted by the European Union (EU) and the Organisation for Economic Co-operation and Development (OECD) following the United Nations Environment Conference in Stockholm in 1972 (De Koning 1994: 72). These principles, described below, became important guides for policy development in the decades that followed.

The polluter pays principle

Polluters are liable for the costs of cleanup and the prevention of pollution. This principle justifies government's efforts to reclaim costs.

Stand still principle

Polluted areas should not be polluted further and clean areas must remain clean. This was to become a major issue in land-use planning efforts to protect clean areas from the polluting effects of sprawl.

Principle of isolation and control

Pollution should be controlled at the site (of industries or landfills) and not be exported to other areas or regions through underground water leakage or through the air.

Principle of priority for pollution abatement at the source

This was preferred over the use of end-of-pipe solutions.

Principle of best-technical or best-practical technology

Best-technical-means technology should be used to eliminate emissions by industry when serious risks to public health were at stake. (This implied that industries should install the technology regardless of their economic circumstances.) Best-practical-means technology should be used when the health effects are limited. (In this case, the economic conditions of industry can be taken into account in deciding on pollution reduction measures.)

Principle of avoiding unnecessary pollution

The development of media-specific legislation, including environmental quality standards and maximum allowable levels of emissions and discharges, thus became the core of environmental policy. The 'polluter pays' and the 'isolation and control on the site' principles legitimised government efforts to require private enterprise to make the necessary investments. Municipal and provincial authorities had the important role of licensing industries in all sectors (manufacturing, energy, agriculture and so forth). The permits issued by these governments were based on standards contained in the national legislation.

The command-and-control approach proved to be quite effective in dealing with the most obvious pollution problems. Over the course of the decade, improvements in environmental conditions became noticeable. Air and water quality improved recognisably, smog levels were reduced dramatically and visible pollution in surface waters disappeared. These improvements resulted from drastic reductions in the emission of heavy metals, sulphur dioxide (SO_2) and phosphates (from detergents).[2] Also, direct discharges of organic substances into surface waters were reduced by more than 50 per cent.[3] In addition, contaminated soils were cleaned up, and new noise-control measures stabilised the noise-pollution problem. Nonetheless, the country continued to face serious problems resulting from the excess use of agricultural pesticides and fertilisers, the continued production of surplus manure and emissions from mobile sources in the transport sector.

Progress was achieved by focusing on pollution from key point sources, especially facilities operated by the major chemical companies and by implementing a comprehensive sewage and water pollution control system. Also, the management of solid waste, particularly at disposal sites, was greatly improved. With the necessary legislation in hand, it was possible to force the major polluters to comply. Comparable legislation and a number of conventions were also developed at the European level to control pollution in the major rivers and the North Sea. These actions reinforced Dutch efforts to take on the large polluting enterprises.

In these early years of environmental protection, add-on technology was viewed as the most efficient method of cleanup. Such technologies, including sewage and water cleaning systems, on-site waste disposal controls, screens to keep noise pollution away from housing areas, and high stacks with filters, shifted pollution rather than preventing it altogether. A major exception, and one of the first examples of source-oriented pollution control, was an agreement with the chemical industries to phase out the use of phosphates in detergents.

Three types of problems emerged at the end of this first phase of environmental policy development.

1   *A lack of shared responsibility for the environment:* This problem called for improved 'external integration' of environmental issues into the regular activities of stakeholders.
2   *A continued shifting of environmental problems from one area to another:* This challenge called for 'internal integration' of environmental legislation and implementation procedures.
3   *A lack of procedural coherence among various environmental laws, which opened up ways for stakeholders to evade responsibilities:* This called for improved ways to share and integrate responsibilities.

To establish the environmental policy arena in the 1970s, ecological objectives had to be quantified. Quality standards for air, water and soil had to be embodied in national legislation. These standards provided a basis for managing stocks of air, water and soil. By passing legislation and setting environmental standards at the national level, the ecological arena was created as a distinct entity.

The Netherlands also experienced the negative effects of this top-down strategy, however. Stakeholders and municipal authorities could not or did not want to be engaged in the process of creating legislation and setting standards. Thus, these actors neither understood the national government's assessments of the environmental risks nor accepted the standards that were based on those risk assessments. As it was believed that the assessments were based on scanty scientific information, many stakeholders and local regulators felt that the resulting environmental standards were suspect. Also, neither the stakeholders nor the local and regional authorities worked to build the capacity to deal with environmental problems.

As a result, the perception that ecological interests and economic and social interests were conflicting was created. It was another 10 years before it became clear that ecological and economic interests are and must be complementary.

Nevertheless, implementation of the newly established legislation was challenged. Private enterprise and municipal authorities only enforced the most obvious aspects of pollution control. By the end of the 1970s, the key source points in industry received permits and complied reluctantly while the majority of enterprises under permit obligation defaulted (Groen 1988).

Still, the establishment of the ecological arena as an entity was a significant moment. What remained was the task to fully engage stakeholders and instill a sense of environmental responsibility. This focus became one of the major elements on the agenda of the next phase of environmental policy development.

The central learning was that all stakeholders need to be encouraged and enabled to integrate environmental concerns into their regular decision-making efforts. This need can also be called 'external integration of environmental concerns'. Yet top-down strategies are required at the outset to define the playing field for environmental policy. Without this definition and the setting of standards it is impossible to identify stakeholders and engage them in policy development processes. At the same time, without the engagement of stakeholders it is impossible to properly share responsibilities for managing the natural environment.

The new legislation focused on water, air, soil and noise pollution, independently from each other. This approach meant that solutions to environmental problems in one medium (e.g. water) often created problems in another (e.g. soil). (For example, sludge from water cleaning operations was either deposited on soils or incinerated. The former caused soil contamination and the latter caused air pollution.) The decision to operate in a compartmentalised rather than integrated manner had to be reconsidered in later years. As such, environmental issues were addressed in an integrated approach to environmental policies.

Sectoral laws relied on administrative and financial procedures and protocols that varied dramatically. The lack of procedural coherence among the sectoral laws and the lack of an integrated approach caused confusion among local authorities and private enterprises. This only added to the perception that responsibilities were being unfairly delegated. From these experiences, the need to ensure integrated responsibilities and design clear and acceptable procedures emerged. This pointed to creating a sense of justice among those who must enforce and those who must comply.

In 1983, the Environmental Protection Department moved from the Ministry of Public Health Care to the Ministry of Housing and Physical Planning. New issues on the environmental agenda and changes to the department's decision-making processes were major changes put in place by the new Minister. In 1984, the department published a major policy document, *More than the Sum of its Parts* (VROM 1984), and the following year released the first in a series of annual reports titled *Indicative Environmental Multi-Year Programs* (VROM 1985). These two publications kicked off a five-year process in which the content and process of environmental policy implementation were upgraded. This ultimately led to the first comprehensive National Environmental Policy Plan (NEPP1) published in 1989 (VROM 1989).

During these years, the boundaries of the ecological arena were widened to cover new issues that threatened human health and ecosystem sustainability. This expanding focus was justified by the public's concern with the slow pace of environmental cleanup, the occurrence of several national and international environmental scandals, emerging public resistance to nuclear energy, and the obvious new problems of biodiversity loss and ozone depletion (De Jongh 1999). During this period, new risk assessments were conducted for air, water and soil quality, as well as biodiversity, and initial risk analyses of global warming were produced. Also, concrete measures were developed to avoid the further use of chlorofluorocarbons (CFCs).

A two-track system for decision making emerged during this period. Track One addressed the effects of environmental problems, while Track Two covered the sources of those problems (VROM 1985: 16).

Track One – the 'effects track' – marked a shift from reactive to proactive policy making. This track translated the existing environmental quality standards for air, water and soil into emission-reduction levels for integrated groups of substances ('theme areas'). The initial five theme areas were:

- dispersal of toxic substances
- waste disposal
- disturbance by noise, stench and external safety (from hazards)
- eutrofication (from the excess deposition of manure to soil and water)
- acidification.

This internal integration enabled polluters to be addressed on all issues simultaneously, avoiding the shifting of pollution from one medium to another. And if emission-reduction levels for each theme area were met, the desired standards for air, water, soil and biodiversity were also required to be met. As the reduction targets also accounted for the environmental impacts of future growth of the economy, it became possible to simultaneously work on cleanup and pollution prevention.

Track Two involved initiating stakeholder involvement in more open processes of negotiation. This 'source track' identified clusters of homogeneous polluters, or 'target groups'. 'Pollution profiles' for each target group were developed. With such profiles in hand, the authorities could show the magnitude of the problem each target group had to solve given the polluter pays and pollution prevention principles.

Under this new track, individual enterprises obtained permits from municipal governments. These permits pertained both to the cleanup of past pollution and to pollution prevention, and included general regulations and standards applying to all mobile sources and waste streams.

The source track was only partially based on direct regulation. It became obvious that additional environmental measures (over and above those required by legislation) would severely affect economic interests for some sectors and ultimately mean higher costs for producers and higher prices for consumers. The expenses for cleanup could be justified, but preventive measures required more from the economic interests directly at stake.

The government then began negotiations with groups of private enterprises. Officials in the Department of Environmental Protection knew that forcing preventive environmental measures upon target groups would be a confrontational and slow process. And business executives understood that if they did not embark upon preventive action on their own, they would sooner or later be confronted with regulatory measures (De Jongh 1999). In this way, a solid basis developed for negotiated agreements between government and groups of enterprises. These negotiations were conducted in open processes of communication.[4] It is important to note that such negotiated agreements pertained only to the determination of measures to be taken and the timing thereof. The quality standards for air, water and soil were not negotiable. In the 1990s, these negotiations developed into a comprehensive system of 'covenants' between the government and sectors of industry.

In implementing the two-track approach, the National Research Institute for Public Health and the Environment (RIVM, an independent research and advisory body) played a prominent role in developing risk analyses. RIVM measured and monitored environmental quality throughout the country. This independent effort played a crucial catalytic function in the risk assessment process.

The more open style of environmental management adopted in this second phase justified a broader set of policy instruments. Source-oriented pollution prevention required new tools, such as environmental care programs for businesses, financial incentives, environmental liability and environmental impact assessments. These new instruments complemented the more traditional tools of regulation and licensing. At the same time, a unified Environmental Management Act integrating the legislation covering each medium was being developed. This law drastically streamlined implementation procedures, and a selection of issues was lifted to an international level. European environmental policy and the Rhine Action program, involving all countries bordering the River Rhine, highlighted the importance of managing transnational environmental problems, such as acidification and river pollution. These efforts also revealed the value of new technologies such as catalytic converters, improved cattle fodder and new ingredients for detergents.

The new approach to engaging stakeholders and encouraging international negotiations was successful.[5] During this period, the chemical sector developed substitutes for phosphate detergents, covenants were established to reduce packaging materials, and the production of mercury batteries was halted. The industrial and energy sectors drastically reduced SO_2 and heavy metal emissions. The agricultural sector greatly improved manure disposal systems and the nutrient content of fodder. Soil sanitation programs were intensified, requiring significant additional funding, and new sites for the disposal of hazardous waste and radioactive waste were established. Efforts to limit noise pollution were also stepped up (see Table 2.2 for additional detail on the environmental improvements).

During the 1980s, the role of the Environmental Protection Department dramatically changed. While the department remained responsible for developing regulations, it was now also fully engaged in proactive negotiations with a large number of target groups, seeking solutions that would be beneficial to both environmental and economic interests.

The one-dimensional approach to environmental policy – the focus on environmental standards without regard to the economy – was slowly transformed into a two-dimensional approach. A clean environment came to be understood as a prerequisite for a sound economy: for example, good soil was understood as essential for agricultural production, and clean cities were seen as having important economic advantages. Of course, the cost-effectiveness of pollution-control measures remained a crucial issue in negotiations, yet the debate on environmental protection now went beyond the single cost issue. Increasingly, a clean environment was considered an asset for all of society.

A number of key lessons were learned during this second phase. First, the introduction of targets for theme areas and the setting of timeframes to achieve them appeared to be significant improvements over previous environmental policies. These targets were expressed in the quantified language familiar to business executives, who thus saw them as just another set of business targets that must be met. In the next phase of policy development, this approach would be broadened and intensified.

Second, the government learned that it was necessary to involve stakeholders and local authorities in designing environmental policies.

Table 2.2 Environmental indicators by theme area, 1980–90

Theme areas	1980	1990
Acidification (mol/hectare)	7,200	4,600
Eutrophication (e-equiv.)	162	140
Total waste supply (billion kg)	47	50
Waste recycling rate (%)	–	61
Dispersion (index)	100 (1985)	80

Sources: Computed from RIVM (1994) and VROM (1993).

As an example, engaging stakeholders in the assessment of risks was found to greatly enhance their commitment to implement resulting policies. Progress was made during this period by 'going fast by going slow', by taking the time up front to work closely with all stakeholders. The establishment of emissions profiles for various target groups was instrumental in defining the objectives to be achieved by those groups. The government's readiness to consider flexible implementation measures and allow reasonable implementation periods was also essential. Because the government was strict in monitoring, evaluating and enforcing standards, it retained credibility in the public eye.

Third, it became clear that it was necessary to establish long-term emission-reduction profiles that incorporated the polluting effects of potential future production growth. The targets needed to include the environmental impacts of future economic growth. After all, despite the remarkable progress that was made in improving the quality of the environment during the 1980s, the gains were in danger of slipping away at the end of the decade. The continued growth of the economy threatened to outweigh the positive effects of cleanup and pollution prevention programs.

The final lesson learned was that stakeholders need to be shown the benefits of maintaining environmental stocks. The activities of this period proved that pollution prevention technologies benefited both the environment and the economy. Many environmental measures either required the installation of technologies that were highly cost-effective (because they reduced energy or materials usage) or created opportunities for improved production and products. As a result, it became clear that environmental quality was essential for economic development.

The major environmental accidents that took place in Chernobyl, Bophal and Sandoz, along with Dutch environmental scandals and the dwindling effects of pollution prevention efforts (because of continued economic growth), underscored the vulnerability of humans and ecosystems to environmentally unfriendly production processes. These developments also highlighted the continued overexploitation of national and international resources. The publication of *Our Common Future* (World Commission on Environment and Development [WCED] 1987) and *Concern for Tomorrow* (on the Netherlands' long-term environmental outlook) (RIVM 1988) laid the foundation for a new approach to long-term management of national and international resource stocks. Both publications challenged society to formulate sustainable development policies for present and future generations. *Concern for Tomorrow* also showed that it was possible to dramatically reduce emissions, increase recycling levels and minimise resource use without endangering economic growth.

With guidance from these documents, the Netherlands was once again poised to upgrade its environmental management approach. In 1989, the Environmental Protection Department published NEPP1, which expanded the focus of environmental management in the 1990s and adjusted procedures and decision-making processes accordingly. NEPP1 showed that it was possible to drastically improve the eco-efficiency of the economy by reducing emissions by 70–90 per cent and stabilising energy use within one generation of people, while at the same time sustaining economic growth. It would not be easy, the report concluded, but it could be done. The second and third NEPPs, published in 1993 and 1998, reinforced these ideas (VROM 1993a, VROM 1998a).

NEPP1 stated that, despite the environmental improvements of the previous two decades, more work was needed. 'We must recognize that the environmental problems in 1989 do not give less, but rather more reason for concern than those problems of 20 years ago,' it read (VROM 1989: 48). It called for intensified efforts to reduce emissions, in view of the dwindling effects of previous pollution prevention efforts and taking into account the projected future growth of production. It sought eco-efficiency levels four to 10 times higher than existing levels for all chemical emissions and discharges to air, water and soil, and sought to stabilise carbon dioxide (CO_2) emissions. NEPP1 set a target for the recycling of used materials at 75 per cent. It also advocated minimising resource use in general, continuing the cleanup of contaminated soils and further controlling noise pollution. NEPP1's targets were derived from an analysis by the RIVM of what emissions reductions would be required in each theme area to arrive at desired environmental quality levels. NEPP1 focused on reducing emissions in eight theme areas, an increase from the existing five.

NEPP1 broadened the scope from *pollution* alone to *sustainable development* at both the national and the international levels. At the international level, for example, NEPP1 sought to improve air quality by introducing stringent standards to curb acidifying emissions, CFCs and CO_2 in the Netherlands. International stocks of biodiversity, energy and minerals were also key areas of focus. In addition, NEPP1 offered three important principles:

1　Material cycles need to be closed (i.e. production chains need to be closed to the extent that resources are not leaked into the environment through emissions or waste residuals).

2   The quality of products and production processes can be improved
    by ensuring that resources stay in the production and consumption
    cycle for the longest possible time.
3   Energy-saving and energy-efficiency levels need to be increased and
    the usage of sustainable energy sources needs to be stepped up.

NEPP1 established the theme area of 'squandering of resource stocks'
to address the issues of resource-use minimisation and product quality
improvement.

The focus of the ecological arena was thus expanded. And the focus
now offered carefully defined targets and objectives that took into
account the environmental impact of future economic growth. The
environmental objectives of NEPP1, as defined by the emission reduction
targets for seven themes (for all but the 'squandering of resources'
theme), were in the course of the decade completed with a number of
objectives set by the Department of Nature Conservation and the
Department of Economic Affairs and Energy. Among them, the
government sought to set aside 15 per cent of the country for the
preservation of biodiversity and obtain 10 per cent of the national energy
supply from sustainable sources by 2020.

The objectives set in NEPP1 were reconfirmed in NEPP2 (1993a)
and NEPP3 (1998a), and thus remained in place throughout the 1990s.

During the 1990s, the Dutch government allowed decision making
to gradually become more open; it granted increased flexibility and
autonomy to local authorities and private enterprises. The objectives
set in NEPP1 became guiding instruments. In 1998, NEPP3 formalised
the government's process of co-designing implementation programs
and co-producing ecological and economic objectives with stakeholders.
That document announced that the Environmental Management Act
would be adjusted along these lines (VROM 1998a: 216).[6]

While the permitting system stayed at the core of environmental
policies, the national government did shift its emphasis from environmental legislation, regulations and permitting to instruments that gave
target groups a say in decision making.[7] Negotiated agreements, or
covenants, with major groups of enterprises allowed private enterprise
to design and time its own implementation plans. In a learning-by-
doing process, a large number of covenants were developed, covering
some 90 per cent of the pollution, waste disposal, recycling and energy
use in the industry, construction and energy sectors.[8] Through the
negotiation of these covenants, the government and private enterprises
began to develop a mutual trust. As trust increased, government officials

felt more and more comfortable giving businesses increasing autonomy. NEPP2 and NEPP3 record this process.

In its 1997 *Policy Document on Environment and the Economy*, the Ministry of Housing, Physical Planning and Environmental Protection reiterated its commitment to open ways of managing and integrating environmental and economic concerns. This document offered a large number of joint programs to deal with economic and environmental concerns simultaneously. Also through this document, the government established the instrument of 'benchmarking' by waiving specific environmental regulations for enterprises that signed covenants and promised to install the best-available energy technology. 'Cost-sharing' was also adopted, allowing groups of industries to establish the most cost-effective approach to implementation within their sector rather than within one company (VROM 1997: 23).

Throughout the 1990s, the government withstood heavy criticism and critics feared that negotiated agreements would always lead to weak compromises at the expense of environmental quality. Initially critics refused to see that these agreements mostly led to results that were better than could have been achieved through regulations, and most were beneficial to both the environment and the economy.

Despite the criticism, a new and more open approach to negotiating ecological and economic objectives had firmly gained ground during the 1990s. As flexibility and autonomy increased, implementation actually speeded up, and the commitments appeared to be lasting.

During the course of the decade, the covenant approach proved quite successful in engaging larger companies, thus reducing pollution from major point sources. Less progress was made in dealing with environmental problems caused by diffuse sources, such as small and medium enterprises (SMEs), farmers and consumers (VROM 1993a: 34).[9] These diffuse groups were constrained by general regulations. The government also created outreach through technology transfer programs, energy saving and efficiency programs, and indirect economic and social instruments. By giving increased flexibility and autonomy to private enterprise and consumers, these actors could tailor the implementation of environmental measures to best suit their needs.

Between 1994 and 1998, the take from green taxes increased 50 per cent, totalling some 15 per cent of all taxes collected. Using these funds, the government professionalised public information programs, improved environmental education programs and established product information systems and energy saving and information programs. Technology development, technology diffusion and implementation schemes became crucial to environmental management.

In the late 1980s, the national government provided local and regional governments with funding to build the institutional and personnel capacities needed to handle environmental issues. By the mid-1990s local and regional authorities were able to deal with environmental issues on their own. The national government thus began granting local and regional authorities the autonomy to set their own environmental standards.

This growing autonomy marked a radical change from previous decades, when uniform environmental quality standards were set via national legislation for air, water and soil. By allowing local authorities to establish such standards themselves, those authorities were given the opportunity to balance ecological interests (mainly related to soil contamination, noise and safety issues) with local economic and social interests. Specifically, local authorities were granted the latitude to deal with noise problems in more flexible ways and to set different soil standards for different sites (depending on the function a site was to perform). Such differentiated standards needed to be made explicit and democratically controllable, and had to remain within acceptable limits.[10]

Table 2.3 summarises the change from 1990 to 1997 in relation to selected environmental indicators. The table reveals that most of the objectives set in the NEPP1 in 1989 have been achieved, leading to a substantial improvement in air, water and soil quality throughout the Netherlands. The construction, industry and energy sectors in particular showed a marked improvement in environmental performance, as have the waste disposal, drinking water supply and sewage and water cleaning sectors. Policies to curb energy use, CO_2 and nitrogen oxide (NO_x) emissions, and resource use are still well off the mark of the sustainability levels described in NEPP1.

During this time, CFCs were fully phased out. Acidification levels had dropped nearly 50 per cent since the early 1980s, mainly as a

Table 2.3 Environmental indicators by theme area, 1990–8

Theme areas	1990	1998	Target 2000
CO_2 (mtonnes)	168	186	162
Acidification (mol/hectare)	4,600	3,800	2,400
Eutrophication (e-equiv.)	140	108	–
Waste recycle % rate	61	75	75
Depletion of water tables (reduction in 1,000 hectares of dry land to be upgraded)	–	119	150

Source: Computed from RIVM (1998a).

result of improved SO_2 technologies in the energy and refinery sectors and reduced ammonia (NH_3) emissions in the agricultural sector. NO_x emissions also dropped, due to the introduction of catalytic converters on cars and low-NO_x heating technologies in homes and commercial buildings. However, NO_x emissions did not come down to targeted levels, due to a rapid increase in the transportation of goods by trucks without catalytic converters.

Emissions of phosphates and nitrate decreased, although not sufficiently to reach desired levels. The emission of toxic chemicals, pesticides and heavy metals (especially lead, mercury and cadmium) also dropped. And if the decline in water tables threatening nature conservation areas had been halted, the objective of reducing by 25 per cent the amount of land area suffering from groundwater depletion would have been achieved. The percentage of waste being recycled is now on target (75 per cent of total waste supply being recycled). As a result, the number of incineration plants dropped; the need for new landfills has been eliminated and most landfills have been shut down.

Further increases in recycling rates will require substantial inputs of energy that can lead to undesirable increases in CO_2 and NO_x emissions. The same is true for soil cleanup efforts. This environmental trade-off between waste and soil objectives and climate change objectives is a case for serious attention.

Contaminated land is steadily being cleaned up, yet the sheer size of the problem (175,000 seriously contaminated sites) means that the goals will not be met soon. The national government's granting of autonomy to local authorities to determine how 'clean' a site must be could help to speed the cleanup process.

During this time period, energy efficiency rates improved at an across-the-board-rate of nearly 2 per cent due to:

1   the installment of best-technical-means technology in the industrial, energy and services sectors;
2   the improvement of energy efficiency in the construction of homes and utilities;
3   the improved energy efficiency of cars.

Nevertheless, since economic growth rates remained higher than energy efficiency improvement rates, CO_2 emissions kept growing. Thus, CO_2 emission-reduction goals were not met.

Problems of air pollution, safety and noise related to air traffic have proven very difficult to control. In the past 10 years, for example, the number of passengers transported through Schiphol Airport doubled to 23 million per year. The challenges to managing this growth are complex, and the issue of energy use and CO_2 emissions by aircraft has not yet entered the political environmental agenda.

Despite efforts to formulate policies to redress the ecological footprint of the Netherlands' economy, the country made no discernible progress in minimising the use of minerals or reducing its impact on global resources. Progress in introducing sustainable energy sources has also been slow, stabilising at some 3 per cent of total energy use and still far short of the goal of 10 per cent by 2020. Moreover, the 10 per cent objective now appears too low to ensure that climate change objectives will be met. National objectives to preserve 15 per cent of the land area for biodiversity preservation are well underway.

As in the previous phases, a number of lessons can be drawn from the Netherlands' environmental policy experiences in the past 10 years. These lessons point to a challenging and complex agenda for the period ahead.

First, it is clear that the ecological arena needs to address cross-sectoral interests engaging ecological, economic and social challenges simultaneously. All stakeholders need to be fully engaged in formulating implementation plans and defining environmental targets. Environmental objectives, broken down for stakeholder groups, are essential to generating meaningful commitments. If such targets are rigidly imposed, commitments are not likely to be achieved in a non-confrontational manner, if at all.

Environmental objectives and targets are instrumental to the process of change and negotiation, and not as rigid top-down guidelines. The advantages of loosening the boundaries of the ecological arena in this way were well illustrated in the national government's success in granting autonomy to local authorities. Also, the covenant process has proven that stakeholders are more likely to take meaningful responsibility for environmental clean-up and pollution prevention when they can address ecological interests simultaneously with economic and social interests.

The development of a second generation of industrial covenants will require the joint formulation of targets for pollution prevention and resource stocks use, including whole chains of producers (rather than sectoral groups of industries or individual enterprises). This plea to open up negotiations does not in any way denounce past efforts to be firm on polluters by both setting standards and enforcing permits. Such approaches are and will be necessary to reduce excess pollution and meet quality standards. However, after nearly 30 years of successful environmental policies that have substantially reduced pollution and resulted in the sharing of responsibility for the environment, it is necessary to understand the perspectives of all concerns and interests at the negotiating table. This will spur individuals and industries to achieve more lasting behaviour changes and better prepare for regime shifts in technology introducing whole new technology systems rather than just emission-reduction technologies. In order to make such major changes, all stakeholders will have to recognise the problems and apply all possible knowledge and experience toward solving those problems. This highlights the critical need for development of technological 'macro' systems for infrastructures for transportation, communication and energy to determine the environmental outcomes of future production and consumption.

Environmental management is not only about reducing pollution. It includes the proper management of natural resource stocks, an open debate and the weighing of trade-offs among all interests and risks. The second major lesson learned during the 1990s is that energy-related issues must be more effectively addressed. Pollution prevention objectives and environmental quality standards have clearly helped to improve overall eco-efficiency levels. Eco-efficiency policies reduced the emissions of most polluting substances by four to 10 times without endangering economic growth, but this kind of success cannot be realised for energy-related emissions. Indeed, the Dutch economy has reached a plateau in energy efficiency. Existing technologies are not able to reduce greenhouse gas emissions much further. Consumers' thirst for energy-intensive products and services continues to grow. And there seems to be a growing desire for larger houses, a greater use of automobiles and recreational vehicles, and greater production of energy-intensive food packages. At the same time, sustainable energy technologies are still too expensive to gain wide acceptance.

A re-evaluation of present energy attitudes and energy technologies is thus necessary. New risk assessments will need to be made jointly in order to move toward a future energy supply and consumption rates that meet ecological, economic and social interests. Energy-related issues require the opening up of the ecological arena to the full range of economic and social concerns in order to prepare for rather expensive, transitional measures to achieve substantial CO_2 reductions and pave the way for even more expensive sustainable energy resources.

The third lesson is that resource stock dissipation requires additional policy attention to be resolved. The government's original intention of establishing objectives for the use of all raw materials and minerals was dropped. It now appears that the poor management of these resources and the huge amounts of energy required to exploit and transport them is putting pressure on the environment, in spite of limited resource use policies helping to spur some progress. Recent research found that the exploitation, transportation, use and recycling of nonrenewable natural resources can be expressed in terms of energy use covering the whole chain. It appears, therefore, that the availability of such stocks is not the constraining factor while the availability of energy is. In view of the limited availability and unequal geographical distribution of clean fossil fuel reserves and pollution problems related to fossil energy use, the Netherlands needs to make a timely transition toward the use of sustainable energy resources. Reducing the use of resource stocks, preserving energy resources and redressing the ecological footprint of the economy demands a variety of policies and poses a major challenge. The government will also need to deal with widely differing perceptions and a great many interests. Simply setting objectives to reduce resource use does not address the valid 'why' and 'how' questions at stake.

Finally, it is evident that major infrastructure development demands cross-sectoral solutions. Infrastructure development in the Netherlands is subject to the Environmental Impact Assessment Law. The procedures that stem from this statute provide a relatively balanced way to deal with ecological and economic interests. The aim is to design infrastructures that serve the economy best and harm the environment least. The proposed expansion of Schiphol, the Dutch national airport, illustrates the inadequacy of a process that imposes one-dimensional ecological conditions on important economic and social interests related to air transportation. Three NEPPs have not been enough to resolve the airport case. The NEPPs' environmental policies primarily involved rather defensive local environmental policies pertaining to air pollution, noise and safety, thus restricting the development of air transportation from Schiphol. The lesson learned here is comparable to historical understanding, namely that ecological interests need to be addressed simultaneously with economic and social interests. Major issues cannot be resolved from an ecological perspective alone.

The goals of environmental policy have been achieved thus far by cutting pollution levels substantially and in many cases through investment in new technologies. This has helped to protect resource stocks and improved conditions for human health. However, greenhouse gas emission targets are yet to be achieved, and the use of energy and other resources has not been reduced enough. Serious threats to biodiversity also remain.

The agenda for the fourth phase includes new efforts to control pollution better and new policies to deal with unresolved issues. The unresolved issues include energy-related issues, the encroachment of infrastructure on environment and space, the increasing use of resource stocks and the growing ecological footprint. These issues cannot be resolved by focusing on the ecological arena alone. Changes in consumer patterns and technology are both necessary.

Rather than imposing ever-more stringent ecological objectives on the economy, it appears necessary to move forward in a new way. These processes need to allow for joint optimisation of ecological, social and economic interests.

Economy, technology and the environment

Approximately 80 per cent of all environmental progress in the Netherlands has stemmed directly or indirectly from new technologies that improved the eco-efficiency of production processes.[11] The remaining 20 per cent has come from shifts in production, changes in consumption patterns and, to a limited extent, a reduction in volume growth mainly in the agricultural sector. Clearly, technology has been instrumental in helping the Netherlands achieve its ambitious pollution reduction targets.

Technological fixes alone will not solve the global problems of energy use and the depletion of mineral stocks and biodiversity. The nature of economic growth must change, as must consumption patterns and societal values.

In the Netherlands, after the three NEPPs laid the groundwork, energy levies and taxes were implemented that significantly raised energy costs. At the same time, Dutch leisure time increased and working time decreased. The demand for energy-intensive transportation, recreation and household heating and lighting grew. Higher energy costs appeared to have little impact on consumer behaviour. Even as regulations, fiscal incentives, energy-saving programs and covenants resulted in impressive improvements in energy efficiency, overall energy use still increased.

Now, economic constraints are increasingly obstructing the deployment of new technologies. These constraints include a threat to competition, at least in some important industrial and transportation sectors.

New technologies are required. New pollution control technologies and devices could become available, but economic, institutional, social and cultural barriers stand in the way of their timely and widespread use. Recent research illustrates that potentially rich opportunities to develop new technological options do exist (Weterings *et al.* 1997). Incentives are needed to provoke and guide the introduction of regime-shift technologies. Such incentives need to go beyond classic regulations, economic stimuli and information programs. In parallel, joint enterprises, government and research programs need to be established that explicitly aim to introduce new technologies and technology systems as well as programs to support the diffusion of technologies.

The *Policy Document on Environment and Economy* cited technology innovation programs as cutting-edge tools for further integration of the economy and environment (VROM 1997). Technology policies focused primarily on the supply side, pushing the development of new technologies. Yet policy instruments have not been used often enough to remove impediments to the introduction of new technologies and the diffusion of existing technologies. Such impediments may include risks to investors, obstructing regulations (including environmental regulations), lack of social appreciation or ability to handle those technologies and a lack of co-operation among industries, government and research bodies. Future technology programs need to not only push the development of new technologies, but also need to take away the limitations that block the diffusion and production of the technologies.

New approaches may have to deviate radically from current production and consumption practices. For example, E. von Weiszacker and A. and L. Lovins demonstrate methods (Von Weiszacker *et al.* 1997) that may be developed that do not require energy inputs of fossil and raw materials and that can be re-used repeatedly as residuals. Such methods are very different from eco-efficient production that reduces pollution levels but relies on increasing the inputs to production. Braungart is correct that sustainable development needs to be more than just sustainable; it must be 'exciting, creative, and fun'. Future technology policy must build on a completely changed public perception of the need to reduce overall resource inputs, not just the need to reduce pollution levels (Braungart 1999).

Economic growth theory emphasises the importance of technology as a driver of economic development, in combination with higher levels of education and improved institutional arrangements. In the Netherlands, economic growth has continued as environmental policies caught up. While the critics argued that environmental policies would impede economic growth, it is no surprise that they were wrong.

Environmental measures taken by industries led to cost savings on resources input and improved the marketing profiles of products. Industrial production increased, yet in a more eco-efficient manner. The transportation sector maintained a steady growth rate, although along changed modal shifts and in improved vehicles, despite increases in excise duties on gas. (The price of gasoline in Europe is four times that in the United States.) The relatively slow growth of the agricultural sector was not the result of environmental policies, rather European agricultural policies and the incidence of diseases such as swine plague.

Consumers have demanded more 'environmentally friendly' products, greatly changed their waste disposal habits and improved the energy efficiency of their homes and cars. At the same time, people are increasing energy-intensive behaviour with more cars, more mileage, more air traffic, bigger houses and higher energy-content diets. These things were made possible because investment in eco-efficiency allowed the country to reduce pollution levels while permitting economic growth.

The experience of the Netherlands shows that environmental policies encouraging eco-efficiency do influence the *nature* of economic growth, but do not reduce the overall *rate* of growth. Projections in NEPP1 that forecast this phenomenon in 1989 proved true (VROM 1989). The environmental policies implemented in the Netherlands over the past decade, some of the most ambitious in the world, did not keep the economy from achieving the highest growth rates in all of Europe yet drastically reduced pollution.

Devising environmental policies to reduce consumption levels or limit the growth of production is much more difficult. Policies of this sort cause serious social and economic disruptions. While it is nearly pointless to limit structural economic growth to less than 2.5 per cent increase per annum – the average yearly growth rate in the Netherlands for more than 200 years – it would be a mistake to put environmental policies in place that attempt to halt growth. The target is to influence the nature of growth, both through technological change and altered consumer behaviour. Emphasising continued investment in eco-efficient means of production and sustainable use of natural resource stocks, and looking to recycling and re-use, can extend the life of consumer products. It is also important to make consumer patterns less resource intensive.

Change must also be based on a broad political consensus. The Dutch experience shows that authoritarian approaches do not achieve the same success as policies produced via a more open style of decision-making. Nonetheless, clear environmental objectives have been and will remain instrumental in guiding the processes of change.

Integrating ecological, economic and social challenges

The next phase of Dutch environmental policy will not be about building new and higher fences around the ecological arena, but rather opening up existing boundaries to assert the common interest. Certain environmental objectives will require targeted attention, such as reducing CO_2 emissions, increasing the percentage of energy produced from sustainable sources and minimising the use of natural resources. Yet these objectives need to be negotiable and brought into equilibrium with economic and social welfare objectives.

The Netherlands has been sectoral-focused in its approach to environmental policy, resulting in a failure to limit the growth of air travel, road transportation of goods, energy-related emissions and intensive resources use. A multi-interest, negotiation-based approach is needed. In some cases, this approach has already proven successful, producing covenants and encouraging local authorities to take responsibility for local issues.

Eco-efficiency in the search for pollution prevention is also a priority, preferably using open decision-making methods. NEPP3 and the *Policy Document on Environment and Economy* set an impressive agenda for expanding these policies in the coming years. Eco-efficiency strategies, however, are not sufficient to ensure proper management of all resource stocks. Nor do they bring all stakeholders to the table. NEPP4, now under preparation, may provide a basis for broadening these policies.

Gladwin *et al.* underscore the interrelatedness of ecological, economic and social interests. They write:

> Social equity and biospheric respect are required for enhanced welfare anywhere on the planet: Improved human welfare and social equity are necessary to motivate biospheric respect, and enhanced welfare and biospheric respect are needed to facilitate social security. Efforts aimed only toward ecological health and integrity ... may produce trivial results at best. Improvements in one area require improvement in all three.'
>
> (Gladwin *et al.* 1995: 879)

When looking at the ecological, economic and social arenas separately, it is clear that they share an interest in sustainable management of the natural environment.

The ecological arena

The safety and health of the population and of ecosystems must be ensured through the maintenance of the inherent quality of the natural environment (i.e. stocks of air, water, soil and biodiversity). Also, resources must be safeguarded from hazards, such as floods and explosions, and from noise and odour pollution.

The economic arena

Food security and the supply of energy and raw materials must be guaranteed through adequate maintenance of the natural environment (including stocks of biodiversity, energy and raw materials). Also, adequate amounts of varying qualities of land and open space, which allow for multiple functions of society (agriculture, industry, transportation, housing), must be preserved.

The social arena

Equitable welfare conditions must be guaranteed through access to work, adequate housing, transportation and appropriate conditions for rest and recreation. All of these necessities can be provided if we maintain the natural environment.

Intentionally, the three types of societal aspirations are identified as distinct areas of interest. Yet all are inextricably linked. The preservation of the natural environment is key to meeting ecological, economic *and* social objectives. Too often, the natural environment is exploited to the advantage of economic interests without proper allowance of the other interests. Susskind has elegantly named this 'the challenge of super-optimization' (Susskind 1999a).[12]

The remainder of this discussion analyses three unresolved issues that will dominate the sustainability agenda for the next decade: CO_2 emissions problems, transportation and infrastructure (focusing on the calls for airport expansion), and the Netherlands' increasing ecological footprint.

Energy production and use are at the heart of managing carbon dioxide emissions and all economic activity and are important to most social activities. Changing energy prices affect the ability of each nation's industry, agriculture and transportation sectors to compete in world markets. Housing, heating, transportation and the production of food all require energy. The increased use of fossil fuels, the burning of which emits CO_2 and NO_x, will continue to endanger the environment. At the same time, an increased reliance on sustainable energy sources like biomass, wind energy (particularly that which is not generated at sea), and solar energy requires the use of open space and may threaten biodiversity.

In NEPP1, the Netherlands made a commitment to reduce CO_2 emissions by 3–5 per cent from 1990 levels by the year 2000. In the wake of the Kyoto Protocol, the target was changed to a 6 per cent reduction by 2010. In order to reach these goals, numerous measures have been taken over the past decade to encourage energy conservation by consumers and producers. As a result, the energy fraction of the gross domestic product (GDP) has been reduced by some 20 per cent. This reduction was not enough, however, to stabilise or reduce annual CO_2 emissions. At present, CO_2 emissions are 10 per cent higher than in 1990. In short, economic growth has exceeded energy-efficiency improvements.

Measures taken until now have been quite cost-effective, with most investments even 'paying for themselves' over time through savings on energy costs. Financial instruments, such as increased excise duties on gasoline and other energy taxes, have been accepted by the public. Tax levels remain relatively low, at least by European standards, and to some extent they have been compensated for by reductions in income taxes.[13]

Today, CO_2 policies will require the deployment of less cost-effective technologies and further increases in environmental taxes. Even if all imaginable technical measures were taken (potentially hurting industry's competitive positions), it would still be impossible to reduce CO_2 emissions to the levels mandated by the Kyoto Protocol. 'Joint implementation programs' and the underground storage of CO_2 (which is expensive) will still be necessary. At best these remain transition measures toward a much-needed sustainable energy supply.

The Netherlands has focused on CO_2 emissions reduction due to the narrowly defined Kyoto Protocol objectives and the desire to produce cheap energy for socioeconomic reasons. This focus obscures opportunities to introduce or develop new technologies, and it impinges on other short-term economic interests. The attempt to achieve CO_2 reduction goals from the ecological perspective alone strains the budgets of both public and private enterprises to an extent that it is not feasible.

However, approaching the CO_2 issue as a purely environmental problem is not the only option. Environmental interests can widen the debate to include economic policy, and encourage an array of technological options for the introduction of sustainable energy provision to the negotiation table. The government partnering with industry stakeholders to learn how best to decrease the CO_2 content of the gross national product (GNP) with the least damage to the economy, or rather in a way that provides maximum economic opportunities, is key. It is also possible to extend the debate to include issues of energy supply security, the external costs of fossil fuels and the potential reduction in the cost of sustainable energies through technological and consumer preference changes. At present, fossil fuel prices do not include external environmental costs, and fossil fuel supply cannot be guaranteed in the future. At the same time, current energy policies seem to assume that sustainable energy resources will remain at rather high prices, instead of accounting for potential technology changes. Broadening the debate to include these economic issues reveals a wider array of solutions and creates a higher degree of acceptance among industry and the public.

The debate can also include social policy concerns. Energy taxes, road pricing, joint implementation programs and other costly policies all influence social equity. For example, money could be allocated to improve access to clean modes of transportation, improve housing for lower-income people and develop cities in such a way that less energy is needed for transportation to work, school, social events and recreation. Or alternatives to the current energy-intensive food patterns might lead to a shift to appropriate pricing of energy-intensive consumption. The public needs to be engaged in discussions about these issues. Such discussions could lead to a re-evaluation of current consumption patterns and allow for the differentiation of relative energy pricing in the future. The debate might also lay the foundation for less energy-intensive technologies and new ways of structuring urban growth patterns.

In the evolving phase of environmental policy, focus on the economic and social benefits of sustainable energy technologies, new investments in infrastructures and alternative less energy-intensive consumption, which will reduce CO_2 emissions while advancing social and economic interests, is paramount. An integrated focus on drastically increasing sustainable energy sources can lead to the promotion of economic growth and ensure greater social equity.

Air transportation has grown markedly in recent decades. Amsterdam's Schiphol Airport is now one of five major European hubs and is the home base of the large Dutch airline, KLM. Schiphol Airport currently handles 40 million passengers per year, triple the capacity of a decade ago, and may handle as many as 100 million passengers per year by 2010. A fifth runway has recently been completed, and plans for a sixth are in progress.

Schiphol is an economic centre of great importance to the Dutch economy. The airport region is attractive to a broad spectrum of enterprises, including flower auction and distribution businesses, computer development and sales enterprises, and distribution and transportation companies. Schiphol provides both high- and low-end employment to the Amsterdam region. The airline industry is also a social asset, offering relatively low fares that make air travel accessible to people in nearly all income groups.

It has been difficult to control the environmental impacts of expanded air transportation or address the public policy agenda. The first two NEPPs scarcely addressed these issues, and energy use in the air transport sector is still not open for discussion. However, local environmental issues relating to the airport such as air pollution, noise and safety are now being debated. In response, Schiphol management has taken steps to improve local environmental conditions. At present, Schiphol has limited hours of operation and the maximum number of flights per year, designed the fifth runway to be as ecologically benign as possible, and banned intensively polluting aircraft. Yet in many instances the airport has exceeded agreed-upon environmental limits. And policies limiting the growth of Schiphol to a maximum number of passengers have been abandoned and stringent noise standards are now being reconsidered.

Schiphol has only partially complied with environmental standards because the economic and social interests at stake are so significant. The need to temporarily close the airport in order to ensure compliance with environmental standards has seldom been made explicit. Likewise, discussions of the energy-use issues relating to air transport are easily shut down when business and industry representatives mention the need to stay competitive internationally. Attempting to resolve environmental implications at the national level is bound to fail. International policies to reduce air traffic by taxing air tickets and kerosene have not been given serious consideration at the global level.

Clearly, trying to curb the growth of air travel would be virtually impossible. The solution lies in accepting the economic and social benefits and trying to accommodate future growth in a sustainable way. This necessitates a stakeholder dialogue, shared responsibility involving leaders from all sectors of society, and consideration of the social, economic and environmental costs and benefits.

An open debate would include discussion of two key assumptions:

1   that air transportation is environmentally inferior to other modes of transportation;
2   that technological changes will not drastically change the pollution profiles of all transportation modes.

At present, air transportation uses more energy per passenger than car or rail transportation, yet is much less harmful to open space and biodiversity. Closer analysis of the impact of road, rail and water transportation on the broad range of environmental resources is necessary. It appears that under certain conditions, air transportation is environmentally more favourable than transportation by other modes.[14] The Ministries of Transportation, Economic Affairs and Energy, and Physical Planning and Environmental Protection could jointly study the impacts of various transportation modes, with the aim of accommodating economic and social needs as well as ecological concerns.

Concerning the impact of technological changes in the pollution profile of future transportation systems, a review of the long-term design of the whole transportation system is necessary. 'Clean cars' will be on the road within a decade, as will cleaner and more efficient rail technology. The deployment of hydrogen planes and zeppelins may become a reality sooner than expected. Such developments could change the perception of the environmental impacts of air transportation entirely.

Widening the debate on Schiphol may break the stalemate on this issue. Of course, local environmental conditions are not to be left out of the debate. It is necessary to manage the impacts of air traffic on local noise, safety and air pollution. Managing car and rail traffic to the airport so as to safeguard environmental concerns is equally necessary. The boundaries of the ecological policy arena must be widened to consider feasible alternatives to the issues.

In the past decade, only modest progress has been made toward ensuring the sustainability of resource stocks worldwide. In the Netherlands, efforts to reduce the use of raw materials in production have been reported, but the effect of these efforts on total resource use is small. Successes have been achieved in increasing the percentage of materials that are recovered for recycling; the recycling rate now stands at 75 per cent (RIVM 1998: 122). A program has also been put in place to preserve biodiversity in the Netherlands by enlarging preserved areas to 15 per cent of the total land area, in compliance with the international treaty on biodiversity. National programs to establish sustainable yields of wood and fish resources have also been put in place, although with significant economic consequences.

Despite these limited successes, increased consumption and production in the Netherlands have caused an increase in the import of raw materials, putting greater pressure on non-renewable resources and biodiversity in developing countries. The demand for energy has also increased. The ecological footprint of the Netherlands, defined as the land area taken up abroad to 'feed' the national economy at home, now stands at 20 times the land area of the Netherlands (VROM 1993b).

Current environmental policies do not address the structural forces that are causing this depletion of resource stocks. Global implementation of the biodiversity treaty is not stringent, and policies to reduce resource use by improving production efficiency have had a limited impact. The majority of the world's population lives in poverty, striving for more material wealth and a fairer share of resources. At the same time, technology, the globalisation of economies and improving trade infrastructures continue to propel economic growth and put pressure on resource stocks.

The Dutch government has abandoned the idea of setting specific limits on resource use, aspiring instead to recapture resources through recycling, improved productivity and changes in relative energy prices to discourage unlimited transportation and trade. In addition, strict biodiversity policies have been adopted.

Gladwin notes that it is impossible to move toward global sustainability without simultaneous progress in the other arenas (Gladwin 1995: 35). National and international interests are inextricably connected making it useful to seek solutions that meet economic, social and ecological objectives at the same time.

More effective policies to preserve national stocks of biodiversity must be pursued. Social and ecological interests are both supportive of these policies. Even in the densely populated Netherlands it is possible to protect additional nature areas to ensure preservation of biodiversity and economic interests.

Policies need to be formulated that will certify the way international resource stocks are mined, so as to safeguard local environmental conditions. The implementation of such policies will require the synchronisation of trade, aid and ecology calling for close co-operation among key actors in each of these arenas.

Technology investment programs need to be developed to encourage the design of eco-friendly products and the use of production processes that insure the continual re-use of materials. This poses a challenge of joint interest to the economy and ecology.

The world must make a transition toward the use of sustainable energy sources. Sustainable energy could provide sustainable growth opportunities to all countries. The fact that by 2010 China alone will emit amounts of CO_2 equal to world's current CO_2 emissions poses a technological and economic challenge. A scenario-analysis conducted by the Shell Oil Company showed that by 2050 half the world's energy could come from sustainable solar, wind or biomass sources. Such clean energy would profoundly change the ecological picture and create economic opportunities in numerous sectors. The development of sustainable energy technologies and a supporting infrastructure is a priority task for advocating global sustainability.

These four ideas comprise a formidable agenda for the next phase of environmental policy in the Netherlands. The challenges can only be met if there is close co-operation among economic, social and ecological arenas. To paraphrase the optimistic messages of the NEPPs and the *Brundtland Report*: it won't be easy, but it can be done.

Redesigning for sustainable development

At each stage in the development of Dutch environmental policy, the focus expanded, the style of decision-making gradually changed, and the array of policy instruments broadened. The remaining unresolved issues need to be addressed by formulating integrated solutions to ecological, social and economic issues simultaneously. The energy, infrastructure and resource stocks issues cannot be resolved from the ecological arena alone. By widening the scope of the problems, a broader spectrum of solutions will be found.

'Super-optimised' strategies for the next generation of policy in the Netherlands could complement existing legislation, permitting programs, and enforcement activities, as well as the use of negotiated agreements and the application of indirect economic and social instruments. The new strategies would not replace but rather add to existing policies.

Standards, goals and objectives for environmental improvement have been a mainstay of environmental policy in the Netherlands. At present, environmental objectives are too narrowly defined and too ecologically defensive. Eco-efficiency goals, for example, are likely to fall short of achieving CO_2 reduction and resource preservation objectives. A new type of objective needs to integrate economic, social and ecological concerns. This requires the adoption of a time horizon that allows for a transition to super-optimised policies and that does no harm to economic or social interests. Such new types of objectives may relate to a timely transition to sustainable energy supplies, clean transportation systems to be developed and implemented, and fully recyclable products with the lowest possible energy input.

Incentives can be put in place to alter short-term interests and induce enterprises to invest in technologies that create sustainable opportunities in the long run. Institutional, economic and social obstacles that block the deployment of new technologies must be identified. And organisational learning can encourage the diffusion of best practice and knowledge sharing.

Along with these things, incentives can be created to persuade consumers to gradually change their consumption habits. An example is increasing relative energy prices through higher energy taxes. A green tax system could be used to promote social welfare and equity at the same time, by increasing the net income of people that adopt sustainable consumption practices.

Thirty years after the national government took responsibility for environmental problems, the majority of those responsibilities can now be returned to the local level. Provincial, watershed and municipal authorities have proven to be willing and able to exercise care for the local environment. These authorities can be given greater autonomy and flexibility to deal with air, soil and water quality and safety, noise and stench problems.

The covenant approach has progressed in such a way that target group management in the Environmental Protection Department can be gradually transferred to related ministries, providing those ministries with greater autonomy in designing balanced sustainable implementation programs for the various sectors. In this approach, the Environmental Protection Department would remain responsible for monitoring progress toward the environmental objectives set in NEPP. The Department could then work more to promote sustainable energy; integrate physical planning and environmental planning into infrastructure development, city planning and nature conservation; and make taxes 'greener'. New forms of collaboration with other ministries could also be created.

The issues of air transportation, sustainable technology and global preservation of resource stocks could be dealt with at the European and global levels. The Environmental Protection Department could shift its resources to address this agenda in Brussels and ensure a proper interpretation of measures implemented at the national level.

The Netherlands gained some experience in super-optimising decision-making processes by integrating economic and ecological issues at the national and local levels. The experiments with local decision-making on environmental, economic and spatial objectives, the negotiated agreements with the industry and energy sectors and the implementation of the *Policy Document on Environment and Ecology* all proved that it is possible to optimise economic and environmental objectives in ways beneficial to both. Also, in 1998, the newly established government earmarked significant funding for the integration of environmental concerns into investments in new economic activities, green infrastructure development and technology. The ecological policy arena expanded to include not only economic interests but all relevant social and economic cross-sectoral interests. This requires new forms and forums to ensure the participation of the broadest possible array of stakeholders for the design of solutions to key problems. The proposals for super-optimised decision-making processes, developed by Susskind, are essential (Susskind 1999a). Susskind's recommendations include the following:

1   It is essential to involve all stakeholder interests in the process of decision-making.
2   New forums must be designed that bring together potential beneficiaries of new policies. These forums must emphasise the search for added value to all involved.
3   Neutral parties should manage and facilitate such decision-making processes.
4   To overcome the problem that one of the groups might attempt to dictate the rules or the outcome of such processes, it is necessary to promote skills of lateral leadership to commit to joint problem solving rather than to a top-down approach of either the economic, ecological or social sides. Leadership across multiple policy areas must be prepared to engage in such processes.
5   Strategic partnerships should be designed and managed, involving groups that have never worked together before.

In review, during the first decade of environmental policy development, in the 1970s, the Environmental Protection Department established comprehensive legislation, set environmental quality standards and developed a licensing and enforcing system that gradually became effective. In the 1980s, pollution prevention efforts were implemented and responsibilities became increasingly shared between governments and private enterprises. Over the past decade, negotiated agreements and the deployment of indirect fiscal, economic and social instruments guided the process of change, promoting the responsibility of private enterprise, local authorities and consumers. It became possible to co-optimise economic and environmental interests simultaneously. Progress was made in improving environmental quality while maintaining high economic growth rates. All these policies must be continued in order to keep sufficient pressure going to promote environmentally sound products and production processes.

The challenge of the next phase of environmental policy lies in maintaining these policies and adding new and adequate procedures for sustaining national and international resource stocks. Preparing for major shifts to new technologies, new infrastructures and alternative consumer preferences is essential. Improved conditions for inherently sustainable production and consumption are needed. Reconsidering the focus, style, responsibilities and ways of working to address the unresolved issues of excessive use of fossil fuels and dissipation of resource stocks are critical. This can only be achieved through super-optimising policies that treat economic, ecological and social interests equally.

Epilogue: the fourth National Environment Policy Plan

Two years after the first publication of the analyses of the evolution of Dutch environmental policy as presented in this chapter, the Dutch government launched the fourth National Environmental Policy Plan – NEPP4 (VROM 2001). The headlines of this last policy plan summarised here are derived and quoted from the text available from www.vrom.nl/international/. The literal text of NEPP4 is integrated into this discussion, demonstrating the plans of the Dutch government to move to the next generation of policy planning centred around socio-technological transition processes in agriculture, energy, chemicals and transport.

The analysis of the plan is that, since numerous countries began implementing environmental policies approximately 30 years ago, these concerted policy efforts have accomplished many things. The burden on the environment has been reduced in many areas, yet there are other areas that national and international policies until now have failed to address sufficiently. Climate change and the adverse effects on biodiversity and the availability of natural resources are well-known examples. The possible health risks of chemical substances and genetically modified organisms, as well as the risks of disasters, must also be mentioned. These problems may have major consequences for the opportunities of people, today and tomorrow (future generations or people in other countries), to fulfil their needs and have a safe and healthy life. Dealing with these problems demands far-reaching social changes, the scope of which is often not limited to one country.

Production and consumption patterns are increasingly international, and with this trend attention is being focused primarily on the economic harmonisation and liberalisation of markets, and less on social and ecological harmonisation. This creates system faults in the current social order. As a result of these system faults, environmental problems are transferred to other countries and future generations.

A new, broader and more future-oriented vision is needed, is the conclusion of the NEPP4. A broader vision is needed, so that it is possible to look across national boundaries and realise that surfeit and scarcity are unequally distributed and ecological equilibrium is being disturbed transnationally – a more future-oriented vision, because reaching a sustainable equilibrium in the long term (for instance, 30 years) demands that choices are taken today. 'Sustainable living' is only possible if there is an end to the transfer of environmental problems. A properly functioning international trade system can help improve this, provided western countries bear the responsibility and costs of ecological and socioeconomic actions.

This approach resulted in a different NEPP, as it extends much further into the future, with a policy horizon extending to 2030. NEPP4 also addresses problems necessitating international co-operation.

This policy document is the beginning of a new policy cycle that sets out on a course towards sustainability spanning several decades. It points towards solutions to deal with problems in the areas of energy and climate, biodiversity, raw materials, agriculture and food supply. Transitions require vision, courage and perseverance from everyone involved. Accordingly, the approach must not be rigid, but flexible, not dogmatic, but creative, and at the same time create the space to learn to deal with uncertainties.

There are a number of important environmental problems that are yet to be faced. These include:

1   loss of biodiversity;
2   climate change;
3   over-exploitation of natural resources;
4   threats to health, external safety and damage to the quality of the living environment.

The desired situation in 30 years can be described as follows: environmental policy should contribute towards a safe and healthy life within an attractive living environment and surrounded by dynamic nature areas, without damaging global biodiversity or depleting natural resources, at present, elsewhere and in the future.

This description evokes several 'quality concepts':

- a healthy and safe life;
- an attractive living environment surrounded by dynamic nature;
- an obligation not to damage global diversity or deplete natural resources in seeking the above qualities.

Although environmental policies in recent years have been reasonably successful, major environmental problems are not yet adequately addressed. The NEPP4 identifies seven interrelated obstacles standing in the way of solutions to the major problems:

1 *Unequal distribution:* Unequal distribution impedes the possibilities for numerous countries to achieve sustainable development. Poor countries often have no other choice than to generate income by selling natural resources, without paying heed to long-term considerations.

2 *Short-term thinking:* It is evidently difficult for people and countries to think of the consequences of their actions beyond the present. Many solutions fall by the wayside because of excessive attention to the short-term horizon. When decisions have to be made, vested interests are given greater weight than interests connected with 'elsewhere' and 'later'.

3 *Fragmentation and institutional shortcomings:* Addressing major environmental problems means interfacing with many policy areas, but the institutions concerned are inadequately structured to find cohesive, sustainable solutions. The same goes for international efforts: co-ordination of environmental issues lags behind co-ordination of economic matters. Due to inadequate administrative co-operation many solutions go unutilised.

4 *Shortage of policy instruments:* Market mechanisms can hardly be used to tackle large environmental problems because environmental costs are not yet reflected in prices.

5 *Those causing the problems are not the ones solving them:* Parties involved in an environmental problem have an insufficient interest in solving it, especially when there are risks involved. As a result, solutions do not find their way to the market.

6 *Uncertainties:* Solving major environmental problems requires system innovation and long-term investments. However, system innovations go hand in hand with greater uncertainties.

7 *Lack of precaution:* For most decisions, costs and benefits that manifest themselves elsewhere or later are not clearly visible. Consequently, adequate precaution is often not observed when decisions are made.

Sustainable development requires a new framework of integrated policy. Social costs and benefits will always have to be considered as being part of the picture. Only then can environmental aims and objectives of other relevant government policies be balanced against each other.

Ambitions and objectives are formulated at three levels. For the long term, guiding objectives are important. For the short and medium term (up to 10 years in the future), a system of measurable objectives must be created (obligation to achieve a given result or obligation to perform to the best of one's ability). Finally, the actual missions are the concrete translation of those objectives to the social players involved. A proactive international negotiating strategy is necessary to tackle a large number of environmental problems.

If economic growth is not to adversely affect the environment, generic government policy is needed that focuses on integrating environmental problems into prices. This will only be possible for international environmental problems if there is international agreement on the objectives.

Precaution is the guiding principle for policy in the field of health and safety, proclaims NEPP4. This means early identification and estimation of risks and appropriate measures, where 'appropriate' means that the risk is balanced against the social usefulness.

Solving the major environmental problems requires system innovation; in many cases this can take on the form of long transformation processes comprising technological, economic, socio-cultural and institutional changes. The period until such a transformation is complete can be seen as a transition. During the transition, objectives are formulated and modified and interrelated policy instruments are applied. Transitions require a type of co-ordination by the government with the concepts of uncertainty, complexity and cohesion at its core. Long-term thinking is the frame of reference in which short-term decisions must be taken. Transition management requires that the government learns to deal with uncertainty, in part by working with scenarios, paying attention to the international dimension of processes of change and keeping options open as long as possible.

NEPP4 provides a complete policy planning and time horizon for *the transition processes* towards sustainable agriculture and land use, sustainable energy and transportation systems. It also launches plans for innovation in the chemical sector and for enhancing conditions with respect to health and external safety.

3 Future generations and business ethics[1]

Over the past two decades, environmental issues have gradually become regular aspects of modern business management. With some success and considerable effort by the private sector, local and regional environmental conditions are steadily improving in most industrialised countries. Changed environmental attitudes, clean-up efforts and pollution prevention approaches of enterprises resulted in a substantial upgrading of the environmental quality of water, air and soil (Organisation for Economic Co-operation and Development [OECD] 2001). Also, waste streams and risk and safety conditions of production and transport are now better managed. The first decades of intensive environmental policies established improved environmental quality conditions for the present generations in mainly industrialised countries. However, future issues involving the preservation of natural capital (minerals, water, energy, biodiversity and open spaces) for the benefit of future generations have barely reached the agenda of the private sector.

Growing concern for future generations

Present management of natural capital casts its shadows far into the future. The rates of consumption of non-renewable resources and the degradation of biodiversity may intensely affect life conditions of future generations. There is an ongoing scientific and social debate on the implications of such resource losses, with varying opinions on the potential threats of such resource losses (Lomborg 2001; Ayres *et al.* 2001: 155; Lovejoy 2002; Wilson 2001). International concern over ecological decline is noticeably and steadily rising, leading to international agreements for the safeguarding of biodiversity and for the management of energy-related issues. At the 2002 World Summit on Sustainable Development in Johannesburg, these issues were declared major challenges facing the world.[2] In philosophical ethics, responsibility to future generations has also been discussed extensively over the last decades (Partridge 1981: 1; Mac Lean 1983: 180; Howarth 1992: 133; De Shalit 1995; Foster 1997; Visser 't Hooft 1999).[3] Thus far, business ethicists have hardly participated in these discussions.[4] In light of the intensified debate over the longer-term perspectives of humanity, the question whether companies have a responsibility to future generations, and what this responsibility might be, deserves greater attention in business ethics. This discussion involves a number of complicated problems:

• What is the specific responsibility of business for the preservation of scarce mineral resources and for investing in a timely transition to durable energy sources?
• How do companies assess and control their impact on biodiversity?
• What views might business leaders adopt in the debate on technological potentials and risks in the transition towards more sustainable production processes and products?

In the increasingly complex and interdependent economies of our time, governments cannot carry out an effective environmental policy that does not have the support of the business community (Elkington 1997). In a globalising economy, conscientious citizens apparently expect companies to take responsibility for the ecological quality of production, near and far, now and later. Companies are increasingly entrusted with their own responsibility to contribute to a balanced social, ecological and economic development. They shape innovations in products, production processes and technology systems. It appears that business is an important, if not dominant, actor sharing in the common responsibility of society to work towards sustainable living conditions for future generations. This was evidenced at the 2002 Johannesburg Summit where private enterprise was actively present. The prominent role the private sector took at this conference differs from the passive attitudes displayed at the conference in Rio de Janeiro, 10 years before.

The private sector started to recognise its interest in sustainable economic, social and ecological development, acknowledging its responsibility for future generations (Jeurissen 2002). Thus, a 'new logic of business' is emerging, in which the conditions of a sustainable society are increasingly understood as the very conditions of sustainable business. This new logic is based on the beliefs that all actions have environmental effects, that human life is biologically dependent on other forms of life and that human beings have a responsibility for the effects of their actions (Freeman *et al.* 2000: 32).

The responsibility of business toward future generations can be addressed from three ethical perspectives: moral rights, utilitarianism and justice. Common to these three perspectives is an assumption of impartiality, also known as 'the moral point of view'. The upshot of ethics is to persuade actors to go beyond their particular interests to a universal standpoint where everyone's interests are impartially counted as equal (Velasquez 1992: 13). From a moral point of view, the interests of future generations must be counted equally (Howarth 1992: 134). Therefore, considerations of the responsibility of business toward future generations can be based on the *principle of generational equality*. The principle states that moral considerations are impartial over generations. Based on this principle, it is possible to consider rights theories (which state that the concept of moral rights can be meaningfully applied to future people), utilitarian reasoning (which includes future generations into its calculus) and justice theories (which maintain that subsequent generations must make a saving for each other).

However, there are important objections related to this principle. These objections are linked to three characteristics bound to the future:

1   the future does not exist (at present);
2   taking the future into account means altering the future;
3   our information about the future is limited.

The first issue is referred to as the *non-existence problem* of future generations. In ontological terms, the future must be considered as a non-being; it is just not there. Speaking about present ethical obligations to future generations is therefore problematic. The second problem involves the effect of present environmental policies on the identity of future people. Taking the future into consideration by taking drastic environmental measures can influence the history of society to run a completely different course than it would run when policy remained unchanged. This brings up the *non-identity problem*, the third problem involving questions relating to information about the future. The fact that there is limited knowledge about the future, and even less as the future becomes more distant, limits the ability to speak meaningfully about moral obligations to future generations. Yet taking into account the objections brought against the principle of generational equality reveals what theoretical defences are possible.

The application of the ethical principles of rights, utility and justice to future generations is illustrated by two practical cases of government policy in the Netherlands, one on biodiversity and one on natural gas resource management. Both cases point to a number of intricate ethical questions for business and its responsibility to future generations. An interpretation of the moral side of the preservation of biodiversity from the perspective of moral rights allows an examination of the case of natural gas management for future generations mainly in terms of utility and justice. In addition, both cases involve different risk profiles that further complicate moral reasoning on the responsibility of business to future generations. The degradation of resources of biodiversity implies rather unknown but potentially high risks for the continuation of life support systems on earth. The depletion of resource stocks of natural gas follows a more predictable trajectory, implying potentially intricate consequences for the access to energy sources for future generations.

These known consequences may be counterbalanced by substitutes for fossils in the form of renewable resources of energy that are expected to be available in the future. The degree of intensity of risks and the involved uncertainties between the trends of degradation of biodiversity and of loss of natural gas reserves differs, and affects the degree of intensity of the social debate on the implied risks of these trends. This requires a more intensive scientific and social debate on responsibilities to future generations.

Moral rights of future generations

The question of what thinking about moral rights means for responsibility to future generations is a key consideration. Ethical theory on the moral rights of future generations, and testing these theoretical considerations, is the focus of a practical case of potential degradation of biodiversity as a consequence of the planned construction of a new freeway (A-73) in the Netherlands.

While Blackstone considers what constitutes something as a moral right with a view to environmental rights, his argument centres on the following (Blackstone 1974; Velasquez 1998: 274):

1   People have a right to a good when that good is essential in permitting them to live a humane life.
2   A livable environment is an essential condition for living a humane life.
3   People therefore have a right to a livable environment.

It is also possible to add the condition that the right of some people to a livable environment can only be recognised when their natural environment is subjected to a serious threat (Donaldson 1989). Looking at predictable, long-term environmental problems, there is a question of serious threats to the inhabitability of the environment for future generations. Long-term effects of global warming, the risks related to the loss of biodiversity and the damage that results from deforestation, erosion and drought are all significant threats. While it might not be possible to know all the needs and preferences of future generations, it is safe to assume that generations of the future will need and want at least some natural and environmental capital, as 'things that they want, whatever else they want' – to use Rawls' famous definition of a moral right (Rawls 1972: 92).

Even on the basis of little information about the future, it is still possible to draw ethical conclusions on present environmental behaviour. For instance, future generations will probably not be indifferent to the degradation of biodiversity caused by the present generation. There is a chance that such qualitative and quantitative losses of ecosystems will affect future production and reproduction capacities, and therefore the quality of life, of future generations. Despite varying risk perceptions on the threats of the degradation of biodiversity and the loss of non-reproducible resources, the international community has decided to take these issues most seriously. Although there are apparent difficulties in gauging its implications, the degradation of present biodiversity resources is likely to affect, at least to some extent, the environmental rights of future generations, and may even result in the destruction of adequate conditions for any future life support whatsoever.

All this assumes that future generations indeed do have rights. A philosophical objection to speaking about the rights of future generations arises from the non-existence problem. What will exist in the future has (at present) no characteristics at all: no colour, no number, no voice and no rights, some philosophers argue. According to De George, that is all there is to be said about the rights of future generations. 'Future generations by definition do not now exist. They cannot now, therefore, be the present bearer or subject of anything, including rights' (De George 1979: 95). Nevertheless, De George believes that 'there is some consensus that present people have moral obligations vis-à-vis future generations' (De George 1979: 94). The grounds of these obligations, other than rights, remain rather implicit in De George's account. He compares responsibility to future generations to the responsibility that parents have for a baby that they plan to have. 'Parents who knowingly and willingly have children whom they know they and their society cannot care for, who they know will soon die of starvation or disease, do not [...] violate any purported antecedent rights of the child. But they certainly seem to produce suffering and misery which they could have avoided producing' (De George 1979: 101).

Here, De George himself transcends generational demarcations by invoking a future-oriented utilitarian argument contradicting his own thesis that future generations cannot be the present bearers of anything. If so, then they also cannot be the present bearers of anything that is to be prevented, like suffering. And if there are moral reasons to protect future generations from suffering, then, within the same ontology, there are also good moral reasons to protect their rights.

Feinberg argues that the non-existence problem does not stand in the way of attributing rights to future generations. The crucial characteristic that decides whether we can attribute rights to something, according to Feinberg, is interest: 'the sorts of beings who can have rights are precisely those who have (or can have) interests'. Feinberg calls this the 'interest principle', and it also extends to future generations. Our unborn great-great-grandchildren are 'potential persons' and the interests that they will have are now morally relevant as 'potential interests'. That determines the present quality of future generations as subjects of interests. 'The identity of the owners of these interests is now necessarily obscure, but the fact of their interest-ownership is crystal clear. And that is all that is necessary to certify the coherence of present talk about their rights' (Feinberg 1981: 147).

Feinberg's arguments, only the core of which is represented here, must be understood at the very least as an important tempering of De George's ontological rejection of rights for future generations. What strengthens Feinberg's position in contrast to De George's is that Feinberg ethically processes the information about future people and about situations in which they could live, while De George ignores it. The proposition that the rights of future generations must be taken into account does more justice to the information than does the proposition that future generations, for ontological reasons, cannot have rights.

Dutch national highway A-73 and biodiversity

The planned construction of a new freeway in the south of the Netherlands illustrates the rights approach in a practical way. This case demonstrates the implications for the rights of future generations of present policy decisions on the preservation of resources of biodiversity. It also illustrates the complex links between national and international policies for the preservation of biodiversity. The absence of sufficient knowledge on the ecological consequences for life-support systems of the diminution of biodiversity renders the development of specific preservation policies a complex process.

Since the end of the 1960s, the Dutch Province of Limburg has been asking for a highway along the Maas River that would provide a fast north-to-south connection: the National Highway A-73 South. As the area's economic potential is mainly on the eastern shore of the river, the provincial government thought it best to plan the highway there. In 1985, the Dutch government ratified this plan. However, subsequent environmental impact assessments showed that the eastern shore option would do great damage to ecosystems. In 1995, the government thus changed the plans for the A-73 to an option to build the highway on the western shore, causing much less environmental damage yet economically less attractive. But after a turbulent session, Parliament reverted to the first option by a majority of just one vote.

Then the environmental organisation Das & Boom (Badger & Tree) launched a public campaign against the eastern shore option. The campaign focused on the fact that the plans would be in violation of European Union regulations and several international treaties on biodiversity. These directives and treaties state that biodiversity must be protected on the level of individual occurrences, species and their habitats.[5] Only when safety or public health is at risk, and no feasible alternatives exist, may biodiversity be affected. The option for constructing a highway on the eastern shore is thus outside the exemption criteria; nevertheless, in 2001 the Dutch government reconfirmed this option.

A plea for the preservation of biodiversity is strongly supported by the right of future generations to a livable environment. The A-73 case shows quite tangibly what it can mean for present generations to take this right into account. Biodiversity is an essential condition for upholding the right to an inhabitable environment for future generations. Despite a great number of uncertainties surrounding the required acceptable or minimum levels of volumes and qualities of resources of biodiversity, its importance is internationally acknowledged. Ultimately it is a question of preserving essential life-support systems (Lee 1998: 285; Wilson 2002).

Because of the scientific uncertainty, it is prudent for the policy on biodiversity to presuppose a precautionary principle (Raffernsperger 1999). The precautionary principle says: 'Where there are certain threats of serious or irreversible damage, lack of full scientific certainty should not be used as a reason for postponing cost-effective measures to prevent environmental degradation.' A consequent use of the precautionary principle would allow the present generation to support the design and organisation of societal processes geared to meet the moral rights of future generations by balancing present and future interests to the best of their knowledge and ability.

Companies and other parties interested in an economically more favourable location for the A-73, and of projects having a similar impact on biodiversity, are challenged to justify their interests and to weigh them against the interests of biodiversity. This justification must be solid enough to address arguments favouring alternatives less imposing on the regional biodiversity conditions. The justification must also be strong enough to hold against potential international criticism of the involved lowering of protective standards. If it were easy for countries to apply for social or economic exemptions to the international rules to strictly protect biodiversity, then this would allow other countries to be equally lax, thus resulting in a spiral of downward adjustments of protection levels which would not be in conformity with the moral rights of future generations.

If companies in achieving their business goals affect interests of future generations, as would be the case if the A-73 were to be positioned on the eastern shore, then enterprises have obligations and responsibilities towards these future generations. Not everything that is economically desirable is also morally acceptable. Society expects enterprises to acknowledge their obligations that are obviously beyond the domain of the direct and mutual business dealings but nonetheless deserve attention of the board of a profit organisation. A first step for the business community involved, therefore, would be to enter into an open debate with other stakeholders on the relevance of the biodiversity issues surrounding the A-73, how this might affect future generations and how business sees its responsibilities in this matter. However, the business community has shied away from such a public discussion.

There are other examples from some of the world's largest oil companies. In particular, BP and Shell have already taken initiatives to monitor and reduce their impact on biodiversity, to drastically reduce their CO_2 emissions and to invest in the development of renewable energy, notwithstanding the scientific uncertainties involved. Apart from these and other initiatives, many business leaders around the world might still find the scientific uncertainty on environmental matters a comfortable excuse for 'business as usual'. It is known from previous cases, like the problem of chlorofluorocarbons (CFCs) in the 1980s, that companies tend to insist on scientific *certainty* before they give up their resistance to regulatory initiatives and start taking action (Velasquez 1992: 258).

The A-73 case also shows that the endeavour to 'save' biodiversity can conflict with other kinds of savings and capital investments. Efficient and effective investments in infrastructure are also a type of 'real capital accumulation'. They encourage economic growth. A society can choose from among various 'investment mixes' to save for a just future. This mix can differ, depending on the identity of the society and its fundamental value orientations. There is no unique formula for a sustainable society; it can have many faces. Because there is no ideal method for coping with the biodiversity problem, there is room here for a weighing of the social pros and cons of preserving biodiversity on the one hand and making long-term investments at the expense of biodiversity on the other. However, the language of moral rights is not well equipped for dealing with this balancing of various societal objectives. Moral rights tend to be expressed and perceived as absolutes that are non-negotiable. Rights express minimal standards that cannot be compromised from a moral point of view (Donaldson 1989). As weighing seems inevitable in many cases, and as rights language cannot account for it, recourse can be taken in moral principles that explicitly aim at balancing values and interests. These can be found in the principles of utility and justice.

Utilitarianism and responsibility to future generations

Utilitarian ethics offers a second ethical principle for assuming a moral responsibility to future generations. In *The Methods of Ethics*, first published in 1874, Sidgwick already posited that a utilitarian would have to take the interests of future people into account:

> It seems [...] clear that the time at which a man exists cannot affect the value of his happiness from a universal point of view; and that the interest of posterity must concern a Utilitarian as much as those of his contemporaries [...].
>
> (Sidgwick 1907: 414)

Here a utilitarian account of the principle of generational equality is presented. Various modern authors have studied the contribution utilitarianism can make to the thinking about future generations (De George 1979; Macklin 1981: 151; Wenz 1983: 195; Goodin 1985). Macklin posits that moral obligations toward future generations can be based on the following utilitarian norm:

> If among a range of alternative actions open to us in the present, some of these are likely to have more undesirable consequences than others, then we ought to engage in those actions that will have the best consequences on the whole.
>
> (Macklin 1981: 154)

According to this principle, increasing the release of poisonous substances into air and water, if it is expected that this would lead to undesirable health risks for future generations, is not acceptable. Even when the discharges have no results for the present generation, it is still necessary to act on the results this may have on future generations.

In a similar vein, Goodin develops a utilitarian argument based on the responsibility to help the vulnerable. Future generations are highly vulnerable to choices regarding natural and cultural resources. 'As long as there remains something we (individually or collectively) can do to protect the interests of vulnerable future generations, we should do it' (Goodin 1985: 178).

Utilitarianism offers a theoretical framework for coherently discussing obligations to future generations. Taking future generations into account not only because of their rights, but also because of their happiness and their vulnerability, is of importance. In this respect, utilitarianism may be even more demanding than an approach based on moral rights. Rights set down certain minimums, while utilitarianism is oriented toward maximisation. Utilitarianism requires that one should seek the best existence for all generations together.

The utilitarian duty to reduce risks to future generations could imply, positively, that present generations develop new energy technologies that substitute for resources that will become unavailable to future generations. Negatively, it can imply that present generations refrain from depleting natural resources that may be needed by future generations, in situations of a technological backlash, where the transition of technologies from one generation to another is interrupted.

It is common among neo-classical economists to discount the future, for 'present goods are as a general rule worth more than future goods of equal quality and quantity'. This assumption would thwart the principle of generational equality, because costs and benefits of future generations would count less than those of present generations. It is important to note, however, that time in itself *generally* cannot be considered a legitimate discount factor. Realistic expectations must underpin any discounting of the future. Risks, for example, will become near certainties if sustained over a long time. Wenz argues that discounting the future may be characteristic of economic cost–benefit analysis, but not of utilitarianism: 'Utilitarianism does not discount the future at all. It does not favor immediate over long-term effects' (Wenz 2001: 86).

Parfit has drawn attention to an ontological problem that poses itself for a utilitarian approach to future generations. He calls it the 'non-identity problem' (Parfit 1987: 351). That future people are *potential* people implies that their existence is variable, both in number (how many future people will there be?) and in personal identity (who are they?). These variables are influenced by what we, the present generation, do. When the present generation decides to adopt a radical social change of course, with the intention of protecting future generations from foreseeable harm, this will result in the identity of nearly all future people being different from what it would have been, had the policy not been changed. Different people will then populate the world. According to Parfit, this makes an ethical difference. People have a considerable margin of tolerance with regard to the quality of their existence. In earlier times, under conditions now considered primitive and barbarian, people did not commit suicide en masse. Their lives were apparently still worth living (Sidgwick 1907: 414). When the planet is plundered and thus provides future generations with an existence that is extraordinarily sparing, but which they nevertheless consider worth living, then, in Parfit's opinion, no harm according to utilitarian reasoning has been done. The alternative is that they would not exist at all – an alternative that they would not prefer. Parfit calls this the 'Repugnant Conclusion' (Parfit 1987: 381). The conclusion is repugnant, because it allows people to do whatever they like to future generations, as long as it does not drive them to suicide.

Mac Lean tries to side-step the Repugnant Conclusion by starting from the concept of the 'placeholder complainant' (Mac Lean 1983). This is not a specific human individual in the future, but a future position that localises an imaginary person who has reasons to complain. The future obligates us in a utilitarian sense because a responsibility exists to guarantee that the 'places' that future people can fill are acceptable in terms of human welfare. Carpenter takes a similar detour around the non-identity problem, by distinguishing between rights *in personam* and *in re* (Carpenter 1998: 289). Rights *in personam* are linked to identifiable persons; rights *in re* are linked to a given situation or condition, regardless of who is involved. Feinberg's previously described concept of 'potential interests' is an example of an argumentation from an *in re* perspective.

The discussion on Parfit's Repugnant Conclusion cannot be settled easily. The identity of future generations is an awkward theoretical complication that is unresolved (De Shalit 1995: 66). Nevertheless, there are good reasons for not ceasing efforts to think coherently about responsibility to future generations because of Parfit's ontological tour de force. One important reason for this is that the Repugnant Conclusion conflicts with fundamental moral intuition that Parfit also shares, which is that one may not inflict just anything on future generations

(Parfit 1987: 388). That is why Parfit's line of thought does not reach a state of reflective equilibrium, where basic moral intuitions and ethical theory convene (Rawls 1972: 48). Therefore, it is necessary to either adjust intuitions to correspond to the theory; or adjust the theory to correspond to intuitions. It is not evident from the outset that the non-identity problem theoretically overrides ethical concerns about the well-being of future generations.

Justice in intergenerational relations

Compliance with obligations toward future generations always amounts to some kind of saving. Whether it be natural resources, biological species or real capital, leaving something to the future requires saving for the future. This requires sacrifices in present consumption. Drastic measures of government, aimed at promoting the welfare of future generations, could affect those who are presently underprivileged. When it is mandatory to bear certain burdens for the future, dividing those burdens in a just way among the present generation is a challenge. John Rawls's theory of justice provides important theoretical insights to tackle these issues.

In the context of his study into the basic institutions of a just society, Rawls also examines the responsibility to future generations. With respect to intergenerational justice, it is important that absence of generational information is one of the threads from which the veil of ignorance is woven. The parties in the original position do not know to which generation they will belong (Rawls 1972: 287). The generational position is an outcome of natural chance that can influence the distribution of social goods (welfare tends to vary over generations, and generations can affect the welfare of later generations). Therefore, parties in the original position, in establishing the normative foundations of a just society, will agree on measures to neutralise the generational factor.

Rawls argues that they will agree on every generation saving a certain part of its wealth for the benefit of future generations.

> The parties do not know to which generation they belong, or, what comes to the same thing, the stage of civilization of their society. They have no way of telling whether it is poor or relatively wealthy, largely agricultural or already industrialized, and so on. The veil of ignorance is complete in these respects. Thus the persons in the original position ask themselves how much they would be willing to save at each stage of advance on the assumption that all other

generations are to save at the same rates. [...] In effect, then, they must choose a just savings principle that assigns an appropriate rate of accumulation to each level of advance.

(Rawls 1972: 287)

Rawls thinks in particular of saving in the sense of investments in goods that are necessary to protect and promote a just society.

Each generation must not only preserve the gains of culture and civilization, and maintain intact those just institutions that have been established, but it must also put aside in each period of time a suitable amount of real capital accumulation. This saving may take various forms from net investment in machinery and other means of production to investment in learning and education.

(Rawls 1972: 285)

'Capital' Rawls goes on to say, 'is not only factories and machines, and so on, but also the knowledge and culture, as well as the techniques and skills, that make possible just institutions and fair value of liberty' (1972: 288).

From an environmental point of view, the preservation of natural resources in the just savings scheme must also be included. The savings mean a burden per generation, in the form of deferred consumption. This puts pressure on the ability of each generation to redistribute what is available to help the poorest, as the difference principle demands it. Generations will therefore have to make a trade off between an intra- and intergenerational operationalisation of the difference principle. They will have to pity the interests of the present poorest against those of the future poorest. Rawls says: 'The appropriate expectation in applying the difference principle is that of the long-term prospects of the least favored *extending over future generations*' (Rawls 1972: 285).

There has been some criticism of Rawls's account of the just savings principle, with respect to his doctrine of the 'circumstances of justice' (Rawls 1972: 126; Achterberg 1994: 192).

If justice requires interdependence (as one of the circumstances of justice), then there can be no justice between generations, for past generations do not depend on future generations for their well-being. Barry solves this problem by abandoning the condition of interdependence: 'Justice is normally thought of as not ceasing to be relevant in conditions of extreme inequality in power but, rather, as being especially relevant in such conditions.' Rawls's account of the just savings principle is not consistent with the circumstances of justice. The apparent inconsistency has been fixed in the original position, where parties negotiate a just savings rate, ignorant of the specific generation they will themselves end up in. Thus, the original position establishes a 'virtual reciprocal exchange' between generations (Rawls 1972: 291). In this exchange, all generations are interdependent, although only virtually. Therefore, the circumstances of justice apply to the initial position, in this respect, and hence they also apply to the just savings principle that is agreed there.

Rawls did not explicitly apply his reflections on future generations to the transfer of environmental capital, but others have done so. According to Richards (1983), the principle of justice between generations has consequences for the way pollution and depletion are treated. Pollution leads to damage and risks for present and future generations. Here the natural duty not to harm others is applicable. This demands efforts to reverse pollution to protect the health and safety of people living now, as well as to take measures to avoid future pollution and to preserve resources for future generations. This implies a double obligation for present generations that, especially in developing countries with a current high pollution load, requires complex investment decisions to appropriately balance the interests of present and future generations. Richards refers in this context to the asymmetrical division of burdens between the present and future generations. Present generations bear this dire double obligation, while future generations may bear the brunt of the burden, without being able to assent freely to this. Starting from the idea of consensus in the original position, Richards considers this asymmetry morally unacceptable. Consequently, he argues for laying the burden of proof on those who advocate a policy that can be damaging to future generations. They must show how the related risks can be kept to a morally acceptable minimum (Richards 1983: 143).

As for the exhaustion of natural resources, Richards considers the depletion of non-renewable resources particularly unacceptable. In the original Rawlsian position, reasonable people will not agree with the depletion of resources by one or a few generations. Being ignorant of the available technology, they will not gamble that substitutes will probably be found in time for the depleted resources. Consequently, Richards argues for the principle that each generation maintains the earth's total resource basis, in which it is possible to substitute capital for resources. To be just, developing technologies that will allow future generations to keep the marginal production of extractions on a constant level is important.

Building on Rawls, Luper-Foy developed the 'sustainable consumption reproduction principle' (Luper-Foy 1995: 91). Pollution and the use of resources are only permissible insofar as they can be continued for an indefinite time: 'each generation may consume natural resources, pollute, reproduce at given rates, only if it could reasonably expect that each successive generation could do likewise'.

To institutionalise this basic ethical principle in world society, Luper-Foy argues for a World Bank of natural capital that would decide what part of the assets of available resources would be reserved for which generation. This bank would then create a free market for extraction rights and would lease the land in the world to the highest bidders. The revenues from this, after deduction of all the transaction costs, would be distributed gradually over all the world's citizens.

International acceptance of the Rawlsian principles of justice appears in the report of the Brundtland Commission. The report of this influential United Nations commission summarised the challenge to balance the interests of present and future generations as 'development that meets the needs of the present without compromising the ability of future generations to meet their own needs' (WCED 1987: 43). This implies the duty to match the need for present economic growth and social development, which depend heavily on the use of fossil fuels, minerals, water and other nature resources, with the need to preserve these natural resources to sustain future economic production conditions. Present savings and investments for the development of new technologies – in renewable energy resources, for example – to allow for a continued and ecologically acceptable economic growth, appear important requirements to meet the just expectations of future generations. In the Johannesburg Declaration on Sustainable Development this commitment to invest in future conditions for sustainable development has been reaffirmed (WSSD 2002).

In the next section the complications of this challenge for the case of the management strategies for the natural gas reserves in the Netherlands is reviewed.

Dutch natural gas policy: balancing the present and the future

In 1959, huge amounts of natural gas were discovered in the north of the Netherlands. In the 1960s, when the post-war welfare state was constructed, the natural gas exploitation was used to boost short-term national prosperity. The oil crises of the 1970s led to an expressed desire to reduce the demand for gas. The depletion rate of the natural gas fields had to be decreased, so that there would be enough Dutch natural gas to cover national needs for the next 25 years, or one generation. After oil prices collapsed in the 1980s, the sense of scarcity as a driving force behind energy policy evaporated. However, the efforts to save energy and to use natural gas sparingly continued, now for environmental reasons. As a result of the international liberalisation of the natural gas market, the Dutch Government's most recent opinion is that it is no longer obvious that the country should reserve enough gas to cover the needs of the whole national market for 25 years.

The original Dutch natural gas reserves, including expected undiscovered extractable amounts, are estimated at 4,250 billion m^3. Nearly half of this has already been extracted, and estimates of future natural gas supplies from Dutch soil range from 25 to 50 years (Dutch Ministry of Economic Affairs 1996).

It is generally assumed that the natural gas profits were mainly responsible for developing the Dutch welfare state. The natural gas profits were thus used mainly for consumptive expenditures. For a long time, the natural gas profits were added to the Kingdom's general revenue. These profits were used to stimulate the economy, to support distressed companies and to finance the collective burden of an ever-expanding social security system. However, since 1995, the income from natural gas extraction has been set apart in a special fund for the financing of an economic infrastructure to support present and future economic production conditions. While this is an important change in comparison with the previous period, it remains doubtful whether the natural gas profits actually lead or have led to an enhancing of the economic structure of future generations. If the investments would have been made anyway at the expense of other budget items, then at least a large part of the natural gas profits were used for consumptive expenditures.

All in all, the Dutch government seems to expect that future Dutch generations will be able to maintain a reasonable level of prosperity without Dutch natural gas reserves and that, from the point of view of intergenerational equity, no problems will arise when the present generations deplete the natural gas reserves mainly for their own purposes. After all, the government supposes that, when Dutch natural gas is largely depleted in 25 years, the Netherlands can switch to imports or will develop other sources of energy *independently* of investments made with the natural gas profit.

Analysing the Dutch natural gas policy from an ethical point of view reveals hard questions regarding responsibility to future generations. The present generations have the good luck of being participants in a technological development that for the first time in history permits cost-effective, large-scale extraction of natural gas. Utilitarian and justice theories both provide reasons to assess these situations negatively.

According to the utilitarian perspective, the gas reserves should be used to maximise the welfare of both present and future generations. Part of the natural gas resources will have to be reserved for later generations, or the revenues from it will have to be invested in the development of durable energy sources, thus creating a 'developmental dividend' for future generations. This should involve more than a policy based on a gratuitous expectation that a steady technological development will solve future energy problems 'automatically'. At the very least, there is a responsibility to invest a substantial part of the natural gas profits in large-scale research into alternative, durable energy sources. The expectation that the market will automatically provide financial incentives for timely development of cost-effective applications of new energy sources betrays a technological optimism that is totally unfounded. It would be pure 'moral luck', if the market provides future generations with all the environmental technology they will need, in time.

The just savings principle reinforces the utilitarian conclusion. Generations should invest in the development of a just and durable society over time. In doing so, they must take into account the lot of the least well off over time. This means not only the poorest among the *present* generation: the consumptive expenditure of natural gas profits for the least well off of the present generation (financing a welfare state) does not conform to the just savings principle. Societies must also invest in the ability of future generations to look after their least privileged. The just savings principle would seem to require reserving part of the natural gas profits to secure affordable energy provision in the future.

Responsible management of fossil energy resources cannot solely be grounded on ethical deductions, however. A natural gas policy that takes future generations into account should also take into account the probability of technological developments. Technological optimists will assess these as highly probable: improved technology will increase the extractable supplies, inexpensive solar cells will become available within the foreseeable future, and energy efficiency will increase so that less energy is needed. Technological pessimists argue that the possibilities to substitute man-made capital for natural capital (technology for durable energy, in this example) are limited (Daly 1997: 261; Ayres *et al.* 2001: 155).

Whatever one's position in this debate, the least that may be demanded is that assessments of future technological developments will not be based solely on personal optimism or extrapolations from past developments, but on technology 'already on the shelf'. Betting on future technological breakthroughs that will help future generations solve problems is equal to testing 'moral luck' and irresponsible behaviour. It is comparable to a farmer who knowingly sells meat infected with bovine spongiform encephalopathy (BSE), arguing that the incubation time for this disease is several decades, and that science will surely have found a cure against it, by that time. (Davidson 2000: 95). The use of *back-casting* studies is essential here – in other words, the backward calculation from a future position to determine how a given technology should develop to allow sufficient potential for this future. There is generally an interval of several decades between a discovery in a laboratory and its large-scale application.

From the perspectives of both ethics and environmental economics, an increased investment of natural gas revenues in the development of sustainable energy is imperative. A societal debate on preservation strategies appears necessary to the interests of distant generations and to commit citizens and businesses to invest in these interests. It is justifiable that the government allocates important parts of the gas revenues to make progress in the design of a transition strategy to alternative and durable energy sources. The private sector will be demanded to be explicit about its inputs on both accounts: to preserve resources and to allow a timely technological transition to sustainable energy sources. Increased efforts for the development of sustainable energy technology should at least prove the standpoint of the techno-logical optimists that it is technologically possible and economically viable to have sustainable energy technology in time. Increased efforts of the government and of the private sector for the development of these new technologies would alleviate the uncertainties regarding the production conditions of future generations, and would thus help the present generation to fulfil its moral duty to demonstrate justice to the generations after us. At present, the Dutch government is starting a process to increase the production and use of sustainable energy, in which it attempts to engage the private sector. Major oil companies like Shell and BP have also started to explicitly demonstrate their commitment to invest in the development of sustainable energy.

The process of the 'precautionary principle': managing uncertainties of sustainability

There are no clear answers to questions on natural capital preservation and the interests of future generations, because there is a lack of knowledge on the potential development of new technologies and of carrying capacity of ecological systems. Neither is it known what the magnitude of the needs and the nature of future generations' preferences will be. In addition, most of the relevant knowledge on future conditions seems to be based in normative valuations, risk assessments and probability analyses of present generations. Aiming to establish a solid basis for policies to protect the interests of future generations requires the development of a shared vision on these interests.

It is complicated to translate strategic objectives on natural capital preservation into quantified operational goals for sustainability. Such long-term strategic preservation objectives are not static. They will change over time as a result of new risk assessments on potential natural capital loss and the beneficial effects of potential new technologies.

At the same time, it is obvious that, if the growing world population is to enjoy increased economic and social welfare levels, it will not be possible to leave the natural capital completely intact. The challenge of passing on adequate natural capital resources to generations to come requires the institutionalisation of continuous processes to balance intra- and intergenerational equity interests. The present implicit acknowledgement of interests and rights of future generations deserves further explication and manifestation. The desire to allow for an adequate natural capital inheritance is expressed to some extent in the 'precautionary principle' adopted in Agenda 21 of the Rio Declaration of the United Nations Conference in Environment and Development in 1992 (UNCED 1992: preamble, p.3).

Principle 15 of the Rio Declaration of Agenda 21 describes the 'precautionary principle' as: 'Where there are certain threats of serious or irreversible damage, lack of full scientific certainty should not be used as a reason for postponing cost-effective measures to prevent environmental degradation.' The precautionary principle contains four different elements (Raffernsperger 1999):

- It is everyone's duty to attempt to prevent the coming into existence of situations that endanger humans and ecosystems, now and in the future. The proof that new technologies are not potentially harmful rests with the proponents, not with the public.
- Before new technologies are deployed proof should be submitted that there are no alternatives to the introduction of such technologies, including the effects of not introducing the new technology.
- Decisions on the implementation of the precautionary principle must be open, well informed, democratic and accessible to all interested parties.

• The precautionary principle is to be employed in a pragmatic sense allowing for reasonable levels of risk aversion and risk allowance.

The precautionary principle has the potential to provide a guidance tool to handle uncertainties in decision-making processes and may provide an alternative for the ever-failing appeal of policy makers to scientists. Scientists can seldom provide incontrovertible answers to policy questions, since they base their analysis on assumptions, risk and probability assessments which leave certain degrees of uncertainty. It appears necessary to accept this lack of certainty, and to design policy processes that start from the basis of uncertainty. Recently, in environmental policy, developments in this direction could be observed. For example, the introduction of instruments such as voluntary agreements, technology assessment programs, parliamentary inquiries and societal dialogue programs on ecological issues are all aimed at guiding decision-making processes characterised by uncertain conditions.

Of course, issues on intergenerational responsibility are by definition complicated by the lack of knowledge on both threats and opportunities. A consequent lead of the 'precautionary principle' would allow the present generation to support the design and organisation of societal processes geared to balance present and future interests to the best of their knowledge and ability. This seems the best future generations can demand from present generations.

Conclusion: a need for new institutions

Three points are outlined in this chapter. Firstly, future generations have environmental rights; there are good utilitarian reasons to take their well-being into account and it is important not to treat them unjustly. Secondly, business has to assume its share in the responsibility towards future generations. And thirdly, there are a number of scientific uncertainties and policy dilemmas that emerge in the discussion on how business should enact its responsibility towards future generations.

A last point remains: that in the present situation the best way for business to go forward is to enter into an open public debate with stakeholders about the complex assessments and choices that are involved in the issues of responsibility towards future generations. Enterprises and other parties in society are mutually dependent in finding legitimate solutions.

Responsibility to future generations is a problem that concerns all of society. Companies share their responsibility for the interests of future generations with other stakeholders. This means that a sense of shared responsibility has to develop. This involves an ethic of the collective good, in which the relations between social actors – businesses, social groups and government – are marked by a voluntarily accepted solidarity with the common interest in a sustainable future. Van Luijk has coined this 'participatory ethics of business' (Van Luijk 1994: 79). With new issues regarding the preservation of resources for future generations, there is a clear need to develop a future-oriented ethic with a participatory character.

The institutionalisation of a shared responsibility for the future calls for a social dialogue on sustainability where business participates alongside parties such as government, non-governmental organisations, religious organisations and unions. Society increasingly expects the private sector to actively engage in such participatory processes to ensure the realisation of an ethical responsibility for the collective good. The boundaries of this debate become increasingly clear with the explicit international objectives on the reduction of CO_2 emissions, goals on transition to renewable energy sources, and specific targets for the protection of natural resources of biodiversity. Within these boundaries the debate will have to take place on the balancing of interests between different sets of people in present generations, and on balancing the interests of present and future generations.

A participatory, future oriented ethic implies a revaluation of civil society to engage in the fulfilment of future oriented responsibilities. Susskind emphasises that present conventional institutions are not really able to handle the complex long-term ecological issues and intergenerational dilemmas.

Policy development increasingly occurs in an intermediate arena that is neither governmental nor private. Susskind convincingly analyses that interaction and negotiation between the government and the private sector has become unavoidable as firms have developed internal capacities for analysis and action. Environmental and citizens groups have increased their capacity to pursue their aspirations outside of state policy.

Von Schomberg proposes a 'deliberative societal opinion development' for uncertainties in ecological and technological decision-making processes in a 'new third arena of societal conflict management'. In addition to the market and traditional political institutions, this arena would act as a third discussion platform (Von Schomberg 1998). It would enrich the political institutional infrastructure with institutionalised deliberative processes equipped to deal with long-term issues regarding intergenerational interests and concerns. Institutions to handle these societal dilemmas could be ethical committees, consensus-building conferences, research meetings, parliamentary enquiries and interactive forums on the Internet. This proposed 'third arena' specialises in long-term planning and deals with the interests of future generations, preventing the otherwise unavoidable situation where such issues that are drawn into the political arena are primarily focused on present-day interests.

The business community will have to engage in these social debates on the development and use of new technology and in the debate on limiting the use of the natural capital supply. This debate will be complex because of the need for the continuous balancing of the interests between present and future generations, in the light of scientific uncertainty and divergent societal views on the organisation of the future. Business ethics can make important contributions to this debate, by identifying dilemmas and underlying assumptions and by reflecting on proper ways of distributing responsibilities of government and civil society.

The fourth National Environmental Policy Plan (NEPP4) of the Netherlands is a recent example of designing practical proposals for 'third arena' type of transition processes aimed at adequate policies for long-term ecological problems and adequate intergenerational distribution processes (VROM 2001a). The plan proposes transition management arrangements to shape social deliberations that will realise innovative technological systems.

NEPP4 has analysed the potential ecological dilemmas for the next three decades and formulates a provisional 'quality perspective' for the year 2030. It shows the need for long-term processes for designing innovative technological systems, at the same time realising conditions of economic feasibility and social and cultural acceptability. The plan proposes to implement processes of transition towards sustainable energy use, sustainable use of mineral resources, sustainable agriculture and sustainable nature management and infrastructure development. The key for action in the short term is the development of a shared long-term 'quality image' that is accepted as a joint perspective (rather than a concrete objective of change). In order to allow a logical sequence of incremental change, it is necessary to define concrete medium-term objectives, allowing a visible and feasible trajectory of development. NEPP4 draws heavily on active participation of the private sector in developing the process of ecological modernisation and of shaping intergenerational responsibility. It is an actual example of 'participatory ethics'.

4 The transition to the sustainable enterprise

A historical and future perspective on the objectives and prospects of the continuing process of sustainable development provide insight into the sustainable enterprise. Analysis of this transition process highlights a comprehensive program for the enhancement of the sustainable enterprise.

Over the past three decades, private enterprise has greatly contributed to the improvement of environmental quality. From 1970–85, private enterprise learned to handle environmental legislation for cleaning up pollution. In a second stage from 1985 to the present, private enterprise has co-operated in the implementation of policies aimed at ensuring pollution prevention by improving the eco-efficiency and resource productivity of its operations.

In most industrialised countries, such environmental policies of governments and the private sector have been successful in realising improved environmental qualities at the local and regional levels. However, they appear too narrowly focused to handle the unresolved global issues related to the use of fossil fuels, and present environmental policies do not sufficiently touch upon the important issues of the volume management of natural capital: energy and other exhaustible resources, biodiversity, nature, space and water.

Private enterprise now engages in a shift towards sustainable entrepreneurship dealing with relatively new issues regarding natural capital. Through this transition process, businesses are expected to contribute substantially to the development of knowledge and of new technologies for sustainable products, services and infrastructures. And businesses will experience pressures to take on substantive responsibilities for sustainable ecological, economic and social development.

Business and the improvement of environmental quality

Several authors describe models of the staged development of the environmental approaches of enterprises. Most of these models show environmental management of enterprises built from defensive, to active, to finally proactive and interactive approaches. The Shell report that describes the process of sustainable management of the firm in its relation with its stakeholders in society going from attitudes of 'trust me' via 'show me' to eventually 'involve me' is well known (Shell International Ltd 1998). Hart describes a model in which enterprises first concentrate their strategy on pollution and waste prevention, subsequently start working on improved collaboration in the supply chain through integrated chain management and product stewardship schemes, and finally arrive at an integrated strategic environmental management approach incorporated in all levels within the business organisation (Hart 1995: 986). Research on the Netherlands' development of sustainable entrepreneurship, as described in Chapter 2, shows four phases of growing environmental awareness of enterprises, building from sanitation and clean up to pollution prevention, improvement of eco-efficiency and resource productivity, and optimised integrated economic, social and ecological business strategies. The transition to the next stage in this continuing process of the sustainable enterprise requires paradigm shifts in the organisation and management of the enterprise. Most outspoken in their observations to this extent are Gladwin (1995) and Elkington (1997).

It was possible to observe a development in the 1970s and 1980s where there was a pressure to work within strictly defined environmental standards contained in environmental permits and licences for operation (De Jongh 1999). Initially, businesses felt extremely limited in their usual practices, and the environment was considered a burden rather than an opportunity. Enforcement of environmental legislation remained a big issue for a long period of time.

As of the late 1980s, the Brundtland Report and many national environmental policy plans dramatically changed the settings. These reports postulate the necessity of a sound coexistence of economic growth and environmental protection. Ecoefficiency and resource productivity became key concepts in private enterprise. In many countries, new processes of governance developed, in addition to traditional regulatory policies. And now, voluntary agreements, covenants, multi-year agreements on energy-efficiency in business and financial and economic instruments form the core of modern environmental policy approaches. Over the past decade, in many countries, industry managed to reduce all relevant polluting emissions by a factor of 4 to 10, and to stabilise or at least to drastically limit the growth of carbon dioxide (CO_2) emissions.

The restoration of environmental quality seems now to have reached levels that provide insufficient justification to allow for unbound intensification of environmental policies. This does not mean that intensified policies are not necessary or not desirable. It is only that above certain minimum environmental quality levels, the right to a cleaner and a safer environment changes in nature. Environmental quality above these minimum levels is no longer an absolute human right to health and safety, overruling economic property rights (Velasquez 1998). Improvement of environmental quality then becomes a relative right that needs to be balanced against other social and economic rights.

This implies that the next stage of the environmental policy of governments and enterprises will differ from approaches in previous stages. Targets for emission reductions or for waste minimisation will guide the corporate governance of environmental issues. And just complying with straightforward environmental regulations will not support the environmental policies of enterprises. Nor will good business economics of cost savings through environmental investments be sufficient guidance in the boardroom. The modern sustainable enterprise will need to engage in new forms of governance involving stakeholders in deliberations and negotiations on ecological improvements relative to and balanced against economic and social concerns within and outside of the firm. A high degree of initiative on the part of enterprises thus becomes necessary to take on new responsibilities regarding environmental and social development.

A historical analysis of environmental policy provides a number of lessons that help to shape the agenda for the sustainable enterprise in the next phase (see also Chapter 2):

1 *Energy-related issues remain unresolved.* Present eco-efficiency policies aimed at reducing CO_2 emissions will not achieve adequate energy-efficiency levels to control the greenhouse issue nor to preserve stocks of fossil energy. Energy-related issues require the opening up of the ecological arena to the full range of economic and social concerns in order to prepare for rather expensive transitional measures to achieve substantial CO_2 reductions of present energy systems and to realise the introduction of sustainable energy sources.

2 *Resource stocks dissipation remains unresolved.* Policies of reuse of wastes and dematerialisation of production through increased resource productivity could not prevent the increased use of nonrenewable mineral resource stocks. Widely differing risk perceptions of the long-term consequences of the dissipation of such resource stocks require full and simultaneous attention of the large number of stakeholders involved.

3 *Encroachment on scarce land dramatically increases.* The encroachment on scarce land, on valuable open spaces and nature areas continues as a result of the growing need for housing, city development, industrial areas and infrastructures for road, rail and air transportation. Both qualities and stocks of biodiversity are endangered. The multitude of social, economic and ecological interests involved require new forms and forums of debate to share responsibilities between governments, private enterprise and others in the civic society. This especially holds true for the development of cities and of 'macro-systems' for infrastructures for transportation, communication and energy, which will determine the environmental outcomes of future production and consumption.

Sustainable business management: changes at two levels

Private enterprise is increasingly willing to co-operate in improving environmental conditions, and not only to comply with regulations – it is now also making progress in this area on its own account (VROM 1998b). Having discovered a large number of self-interested economic motives, enterprise is adopting a proactive stance towards the environment. Important motivating economic arguments include opportunities to cut on costs by saving energy, water, mineral resources and packaging materials. An enhanced marketing profile towards customers who are demanding cleaner products and production processes is also important. Facing banks and insurance companies demanding the highest environmental standards of companies they supply with investment capital and insurance services is another consideration.

These present changes appear to be more fundamental than those made previously. The environmental effects of modern production processes spill over to geographical levels and have consequences on time scales that are far from both the place and time in which they originate. The nationally bounded government as the natural caretaker of the free market and governor of economic, social and ecological interests is losing its influence and capacity to control such impacts

(Kennedy 1993). Governments increasingly need to share these responsibilities with the private sector, and companies experience a growing self-interest in protecting and developing the quality of and access to natural capital as a prime condition for production, both nationally and internationally.

Non-governmental organisations (NGOs) active in environmental and nature protection, or in socioethical fields, have experienced an increased influence on both governments and private enterprise at the national and international level. A fundamental shift is taking place in which new roles are taken up by private enterprise and by organisations of civic society at the expense of the traditional regulating functions of governments. The example of Shell and the Brent Spar is already legendary, and is only one example.

Government policies of regulation and of fiscal and economic stimulation are increasingly supplemented by external environmental pressures in markets. Customers, financial partners and NGOs exert new pressures on companies to take on such social and ecological responsibilities. Also, there are increasing pressures from within the firms themselves and from the business chains they are operating in. Companies have become vulnerable, and are increasingly aware of their dependence on other businesses in the production chain and of their shared responsibility.

The preservation of natural capital – minerals, energy, water and biodiversity – has now slowly entered the political agenda. The private sector is as yet hardly involved. Its role, however, is crucial as it holds the keys to technological modernisation of production processes and of products and services. Explicitly assuming responsibility for the creation of adequate future production conditions as part of the core ideology of the firm gives companies strategic guidance. There are a growing number of companies that include long-term ecological concerns in their core strategies. There is also a tendency among private businesses to actively participate in the societal debate on ecological and socioeconomic modernisation, in particular with respect to the accountability of business activities affecting long-term conditions for production and reproduction. Enterprises want to avoid surprises and prepare anticipatory and future-oriented actions. They want to be able to influence the strategic conditions for business. It is this long-term perspective that motivates the management of sustainable companies and that equips them to adequately deal with changes in the strategic long-term conditions of the firm (Collins and Porras 1996).

The 'licence to operate' – or, *a fortiori,* 'the licence to grow' – of a company is not a static entity, but concerns a dynamic set of conditions requiring continuous maintenance. Sustainability requires corporate sustainability management to be amended at two distinct levels (Social Economic Council [SEC] 2001).

The first level concerns the daily governance of the firm itself, where new environmental demands come forward from outside (the market and government regulations), from within the company, and from business relations in the business chain (Kolk 2000). The second level relates to the need for companies to substantively contribute to the maintenance and improvement of the social, economic, technological and infrastructural production conditions of the firm. The ebbing influence of governments, the globalisation of economies and the internationalisation of social and environmental standards demand private enterprise to take initiative to sustain its future competitive advantage. Private enterprise will experience new tasks in contributing to the development of sustainable energy and transport infrastructures, and in designing and implementing new sustainable technologies. At both levels, internally and externally, the sustainable enterprise faces new challenges.

Business and the management of natural capital

The first stage of environmentally friendly production, contributing to the improvement of the quality of natural capital, of water, air, soil, nature, biodiversity and space, is complete. Today a new phase is beginning with attention focused on the preservation of quantities or stocks of natural capital, including the conservation of fossil fuels, mineral resources, biodiversity, water and space. This preservation relates not only to the tangible interests of the present generation, but also to future generations. The inevitable intensification of the use of natural capital demands a careful transition towards new conditions for the use of resource stocks.

At present, the focus of companies is on eco-efficiency, mainly pertaining to the reduction of polluting emissions and rather than the need to increase resource productivity and decrease land use to preserve nature and stocks of biodiversity. New technologies to minimise the input of mineral resources, to reduce pressure on land, and to ensure the timely transition to sustainable energy technologies, are at the core of factor 10 analyses, as proclaimed in, for example, the Carnoules Declaration.[1] Such issues of sustainability go beyond the traditional improvement of environmental quality and direct intensive attention to the preservation of stocks of natural capital for future generations.

The world population is expected to double in size over the next 40 or 50 years, and to stabilise at a level of some 10 billion people. During this same period, total economic production will increase fivefold. Energy consumption may grow to three times the present levels and food production will double. By 2040, everywhere in the world, except in Africa, material welfare levels can be achieved that compare to average European levels of the past decade (United Nations Environment Programme [UNEP] 1997: 218). Large economic and social inequities within and between countries can disappear. However, if environmental policies remain unaltered, these favourable economic and social trends will have strong environmental impacts. They will cause dramatic climatic changes, energy resources will rapidly dissipate and mineral resources will convert into waste. The world forest reserves could be cut by 25 per cent and the quality and quantities of biodiversity could dramatically decline (Rotmans and De Vries 1997).

From fundamental food production theory it is known that the planet can provide food for many times the present size of the world's population (WRR [Netherlands Scientific Council for Government Policy] 1995: 49). And society can develop technologies and processes to establish adequate sustainable yields of wood and other renewable resources, and keep mineral resources in the production chain. In addition, society is learning how to clean polluted waters and soils, and how to prevent pollution. So the planet earth is not a finite stock, but a dynamic resources system with incredible potentials for production and reproduction, and open to the influx of solar energy (Ayres 1998). As long as the dynamics of the system are protected, reusing its stocks of natural capital will be possible. This will allow future generations sufficient potential for production and reproduction, and balance social, economic and ecological interests at increased levels. In this sense it is possible to reconsider the urgent messages of the Club of Rome of 1972. Clearly, stringent conditions for and principles of production need to be met to allow continuation of the progress realised to date and to be able to achieve the prospects of sustainable development.

Ekins recently summarised these stringent conditions for and principles of sustainable development as developed in past economic research on sustainable development by pioneers such as Daly, Pearce and Turner (Ekins 2000: 95).

1 Prevent destabilisation of global climate patterns and the ozone layer.
2 Protect ecosystems and maintain biological diversity.

3   Foster the reproduction of renewable resources by realising sustainable yields.
4   Balance the depletion of exhaustible resources with the development of substitutes.
5   Do not allow emissions of air, soil and water to exceed the critical load of the receiving media.
6   Preserve landscapes of special human and ecological significance.
7   Keep risks of life-damaging results from human events at very low levels.

Such recommendations are indispensable in designing policies and practices for sustainable enterprise. They guide the development of operational environmental policies of governments and help private enterprise in the design of practical sustainable business strategies. Pioneering authors as, for example, Paul Hawken, Amory and Hunter Lovins, John Elkington and Stuart Hart, and institutions such as the Factor 10 Club, the World Business Council for Sustainable Development and the Natural Step, are translating these principles into practical guidelines to enhance the formulation of sustainable business strategies (Hawken 2000: 10).

In several respects, these principles and guidelines of sustainable development appear to be too static, leaving not enough room for inevitable trade-off processes both at the macro-level as well as at the micro-level of the firm.

1   The principles of sustainable production are basically long-term strategic objectives. It is very complicated to translate these strategic objectives into operational goals for the sustainable enterprise. Also, such long-term strategic objectives are not static. They will change over time as a result of new risk assessments of the consequences of losses of natural capital and of the potential beneficial effects of potential new technologies. Hence, there will be continuous trade-off processes around the translation of long-term strategic objectives into short-term operational goals.
2   The listed recommendations give prime focus to the environmental and economic aspects of sustainable development. This dominant environmental focus does not allow for the adequate balancing of social, economic and ecological interests. It is obvious that for the growing world population to enjoy increased economic and social welfare levels, it will not be possible to leave the natural capital completely intact. Hence, trade-offs between social, economic and

ecological interests are inevitable and processes to allow for such decisions need to be designed.

3 The listed principles do not make a proper distinction between renewable resource stocks, such as minerals and water, and nonrenewable resource stocks of fossil fuels, biodiversity and space. In all forms of production the input of these 'key stocks' are used: energy, biodiversity and land (VROM 1995). Hence, balancing the use of non-renewable 'key stocks' and of economic and social development will be inevitable.

While recycling and reuse of exhaustible but renewable resources can be brought back into the production cycle, this is not the case with 'key stocks' of fossil energy, biodiversity and land, which are nonrenewable. These resources cannot be recycled and reused, and in this respect are fundamentally different from resources like minerals and water. The nature of nonrenewable resources is the reason to identify them as the 'key stocks' of natural capital. The 'key stocks' also differ from other exhaustible resources, since they serve as auxiliary resources in the recycling of exhaustible resources and renewable resources, and for the cleaning of polluted environmental resources. With the aid of the 'key stocks' all other resources can be regained.

The preservation of these 'key stocks', which by definition form the limits to growth, deserves prime attention in the next stage of policies of sustainable development and of sustainable entrepreneurship (VROM 1999). Preservation of the 'key stocks' of space will be served by using methods of compact building over ground or underground, and through the development of underground infrastructures. By creating space for nature development, the dynamics of the key stock of biodiversity can be restored and maintained.

The sustainable enterprise is about business processes that not only reduce emissions, and ensure reuse of renewable and recyclable resource stocks, but also allow for the preservation of the key stocks of natural capital. At the same time the sustainable enterprise works to allow adequate social and economic development, both nationally and internationally. However, there are strategic problems related to the key stocks of energy, space and biodiversity which both governments and the private sector need to face.

The example of the rapid depletion of the extensive natural gas reserves in the Netherlands was already outlined in detail in the previous chapter. It presents questions of whether the Netherlands should conserve its stocks of natural gas or, alternatively, utilise the gas profits fully for the development of sustainable energy sources.

As another example, together with Hong Kong and Singapore, the Netherlands shares the top positions on the list of the most densely populated countries in the world. Accommodating the expected growth of its population from 16 to 18 million along the present average land use per capita, or intensifying efforts to build expensive space saving over-ground and underground facilities, are complicated issues. With these examples, a new dilemma on energy intensity versus land intensity of production emerges, putting additional pressure on the need to search for substitutes for exhaustible energy and land resources.

Private enterprise will increasingly and intensively be confronted with such new responsibilities and liabilities. The United Nations Conference on Environment and Development (UNCED) Agenda 21 and the Biodiversity Treaty of Rio de Janeiro of 1992, and in their wake the (European) laws on the reservation of land for the protection of ecospecies, gradually translate into national and regional land use plans that make severe impositions on economic activities. Also in the field of energy use, the Kyoto Protocol now translates into national energy plans that seriously affect the traditionally free opportunities for the use of energy, implying a reduction of the average national fossil fuel intensity of gross domestic product by 50 per cent within 30 years.

These agreements put an enormous burden on society and pose a huge technological challenge to private enterprise. They require a fundamental change of technologies for energy use in production processes, a dramatic change of the energy content of the consumer package, and restrictions on land use.

After a long period where the prime focus of governments and private enterprise was on improving environmental quality conditions, now key issues on the preservation of resource stocks rapidly come to the front. Much sooner than anticipated by private enterprise, transitions are required to new forms of (underground) land use and to sustainable energy sources. The debate on the transition to sustainable energy resources and to technologies that severely limit the use of land and space will soon dominate the agenda of the sustainable enterprise.

The strategic issues on the use of the key stocks of natural capital and the need to develop substitutes or alternatives will become increasingly urgent. It is not possible to avoid losses on the reserves of these key stocks, but substitutes and alternatives can be developed, and decisions need to be made on the extent that either of these stocks should be preserved at the expense of the others. There is an ongoing and controversial academic debate of neo-classical economists, like Solow, and ecological economists, like Daly, on the extent to which ecological processes and available resource stocks pose limits on the potentials for economic growth (Daly 1997: 261). This debate is the clear manifestation of the inevitable trade-offs that need to be made. Trade-offs, balancing various societal goals of economic continuity and growth, of increased social welfare, of improved environmental quality conditions, and of desires to preserve resources of natural capital for future generations, will be inevitable and will be continuously at stake. All these interests are inextricably connected and the balanced satisfaction of each of the interests is needed to allow advances in all respects.

The next stage of sustainability and of the sustainable enterprise requires additional tools and targets to guide the private sector towards more sustainable practices. And the next stage also requires the active and constructive participation of enterprises in the societal dialogue seeking an adequate balance of economic, ecological and social interests of present and future generations.

Building on the rules of Daly, Pearce, Turner and Hawken, the requirements of sustainable management of natural capital are outlined as follows:

1   Natural capital requires quality management to the extent that its reproduction capacities and reusability of its resource stocks are least affected.
2   Fossil energy, biodiversity and high quality areas of space are finite and non-reproducible 'key stocks' of natural capital and must for those reasons be preserved as much as possible for future generations. The use of these 'key stocks', in whatever composition, is inevitable. Their use, however, can and should be minimised with substitute resources like sustainable energies and alternative uses of land.
3   Corporate governance of the sustainable enterprise requires its active and constructive participation in the societal dialogue on balancing social, economic and ecological interests.

Yet the question of why private enterprise needs to alter present attitudes and shift towards the alleviation of social, economic and ecological pressures remains. A related question is why private enterprise needs to develop new technologies for the preservation of key stocks of natural capital, and become more actively engaged in the societal management of social-economic issues. Amartya Sen points to both economic and ethical arguments, recognising the self-interest of private enterprise to safeguard continued and appropriate conditions for production in terms of access to land, energy and other resources for production. He also acknowledges the increasing pressures on quality and availability, and thus on the distribution of and access to (international) public goods. In order to reduce the regulating tasks of governments in achieving fair access to scarce common resources and public goods, he strongly favours the development of an ecological ethic in private enterprise by demanding the achievement of strong ethical standards and of a strong sense of responsibility of private enterprise with respect to the preservation of natural capital (Sen 1999: 258).

The ethical question of whether enterprises do have obligations or responsibilities towards future generations thus is an important one for economists, as was extensively discussed in the previous chapter, and the debate continues about the optimal use of natural capital and on the substitution possibilities of natural capital for social and economic capital. The debate centres on varying assumptions about the level at which people are adequately able to define responsibilities on the preservation of natural capital into their preferences. Discussion also pertains to the level that the development of technology can and will provide substitutes for exhaustible resources, energy and space. As mentioned in the previous section, it is necessary to transcend such academic debates and enter into explicit societal debates on future social, economic and ecological liabilities.

The entitlement to the heritage of the 'common patrimony' is an accepted concept in Agenda 21 established in 1992 at the UNCED of Rio de Janeiro, and obliges present generations to leave sufficient resource stocks of natural capital (UNCED 1992). Even if it would be possible to implement the mastered technologies to achieve sustainable yields of reproducible resource stocks, and continue to recycle and recover exhaustible resource stocks, this would leave the inevitable loss of reserves of key stocks of natural capital: fossil energy, biodiversity and space. Although sustainable substitutes for energy and for use of land do become available, it will be impossible to pass on present stocks of natural capital. Hence, a careful balance in the development of social and economic capital against the preservation of stocks of natural capital must be established. According to Rawls' principle of 'justice as fairness', the key stocks should not be depleted to the extent that production and reproduction capacities of future generations decline to less than present production levels. Rich countries therefore have special responsibilities as they already have constituted relatively just social and economic capital levels. Moreover, these countries are in a position to afford the development of knowledge and technologies that contribute to production methods that can save on key stocks and substitute for traditional energy and land-intensive production procedures.

The United Nations' Agenda 21, the Treaty on Biodiversity, the Kyoto Protocol and numerous national environmental and nature plans detail the common responsibility to preserve reserves of natural capital for future generations. Yet questions remain as to who is actually liable, and what the role of sustainable enterprise will be.

If companies attempting to achieve their business goals touch upon interests of future generations, then enterprises have obligations and responsibilities towards these future generations. Van Luijk and Schilder (1997) propose that society expects enterprises to acknowledge their obligations which are obviously beyond the domain of the direct and mutual business dealings but nonetheless deserve attention of the board of a profit organisation (i.e. issues regarding the interests of future generations, the environment and the less fortunate in society).

Certainly, responsibilities for future generations are the concern of society as a whole. The ethics of managing public goods is characterised by a voluntarily accepted solidarity for the common cause. These ethics are participatory in nature. Unlike the currently separated responsibilities of governments and the private sector in governing society, this demands a collective responsibility of and close co-operation between all societal parties (Sen 1999: 256). Enterprises and other parties in society are mutually dependent in finding solutions for the dilemmas involved. They are stakeholders in the same dilemmas and are jointly responsible. Van Luijk explains this call for participatory ethics as follows:

> ... a company can not be made accountable to any project it may have engaged itself in. But if a company does not want to be accountable for anything at all, when it consequently refuses any societal participation, then this company can be accused of moral neglect.
>
> (Van Luijk 1993: 53)

The concept of 'participatory ethics' calls for processes that engage enterprises in the sharing of responsibilities. Two matters demand full attention (see also Chapter 3):

- Consensus building and conflict management: how can a plane be created that carries the required changes to allow for proper intra- and intergenerational responsibility?
- Transition management: policy developments and societal paradigm shifts to explicitly include intergenerational responsibilities.

Changing conditions for the 'licence to operate'

The development of the sustainable enterprise is taking place under dynamic social, economic and technological circumstances that are demanding and promising. In recent literature such intensive changes have been identified as important paradigm shifts for enterprises:[2]

- *Globalisation of economies:* Increasing international economic relations and activities of enterprises have increasing environmental impacts through the intensified use of natural resources and increased transport movements. But, also, there is a tendency to a global standardisation of ecological and social standards.
- *Technological revolution:* Technological renewals shift from eco-efficient and resource productive technologies aimed at minimising environmental impacts towards sustainable energy, transportation, construction, agricultural and chemical technologies aimed at preserving natural capital. Continuous innovation through product stewardship programs and intensified collaboration in technology chains may improve the environmental impact of economic development.
- *Market conditions for sustainability:* Not everything that is statutorily allowed is now acceptable in markets. Purchasing parties in markets, whether they are private customers, governments or private enterprise relations, set increasingly higher social and environmental standards. Competition on the ecological status of new products and production processes grows steadily in importance.
- *Sustainability management changes:* Companies are globally answerable on the quality of their operations. The increasing transparency of business activities encompasses their actions regarding human rights, health and safety standards and environmental performance, and businesses will also become explicitly accountable on the preservation of natural capital.

These changing conditions demand responses in business strategies. They also provide opportunities for the development of new products and production processes and provide challenges to open new markets.

This process of transition will continue for decades and it is evident that individual companies can only partially influence it. Yet the individual and combined potentials for change of the private sector must not be underestimated. Over the past decades, private enterprise jointly managed an environmental transition by improving eco-efficiency and resource productivity of production, greatly contributing to the restoration and conservation of environmental qualities. This resulted in a gradual shift from taking on responsibilities at the level of individual companies (complying with licences and permits) towards voluntary environmental arrangements between the government and groups of enterprises. Now there are environmental covenants with whole branches, chain responsibilities linking companies in all aspects of production from cradle to grave, and sector-wide arrangements on energy-saving measures and certification (VROM 1998a).

The private sector now faces a new challenge. It is not just sectors, branches or companies in the same production chain but private sector as a whole that will need to be involved in the transition towards sustainability. Technological renewal and technology transitions are key to the preservation of natural capital. In designing these new technologies it will be necessary to configure new alliances of established and new companies that go beyond the traditional networks of enterprises and supersede traditional competitive relations. Transitions towards new systems of technology require new alliances. Such new responsibilities for private enterprise can only be established in an intensive societal debate on modernisation of technology and improved infrastructural conditions. Organised society-wide processes of consensus building appear necessary to set out these responsibilities and, also, to show and to develop new opportunities for business (Susskind 1999a).

In a historical perspective, established enterprises have not been successful in making radical shifts to new technologies and production systems. Ashford points to the risk-aversion attitudes of those with vested interests in large industries and also concludes that, when environmental improvement becomes a centrepiece for industry as a whole, risks can be reduced and shared. He proposes strategies of innovation that simultaneously address the willingness, capacity and opportunity to change (Ashford 1994). Hart equally emphasises the need for private enterprise to jointly take on the challenge of sustainability, which contains both risks and opportunities (Hart and Milstein 1999: 23). The inevitable process of creative destruction will prove profitable if managers analyse the opportunities from the market perspective, Hart argues. He shows the varying and differing business opportunities for sustainability in industrialised economies, newly industrialising economies, and in 'survival' economies of the poorer countries in the world. Technological innovation strategies differ extensively for the market approaches by business in these different economies, yet show excellent opportunities for established enterprises as well as for newly developing companies. Shared undertakings of established and new businesses will pave the way to fully absorbing the opportunities for renewal, reducing the risks at the same time. Gladwin states that: 'For corporations, supposedly chartered by and accountable to citizens, sustainability implies nothing less than a radical redefinition of the social contract that business maintains with society' (Gladwin 1995: 35).

An impressive move towards sustainable entrepreneurship has been made so far:

- Over the past decades the private sector has made a substantial contribution to the improvement of environmental quality all around the industrialised world. However, future-oriented issues involving natural capital resource preservation (minerals, water, energy, biodiversity and land use) for the benefit of future generations have barely reached the agenda of the private sector. Enterprises should prepare to engage in discussions about these future issues that will rapidly enter the entrepreneurial agenda.
- Enterprises have an important role in the development of future societal conditions. They shape innovation in products, production processes and technology systems and hold the key for innovation. Companies are co-responsible for the promotion of interests of present and future generations. They can be held accountable for such responsibilities.
- The private sector does not have to bear these future-oriented responsibilities alone. They share them with other parties in society: governments and societal organisations. However, enterprises will be asked to co-shape processes to address future-oriented responsibilities. Companies also have a business economic self-interest in active participation in the societal debate.
- Governments are shaping processes of ecological, social, economic and technological modernisation, carefully balancing widely differing interests within present generations and between present and future generations. Technological innovation is very much needed to allow a growing space to match and meet all these different interests. Joint consensus-building processes will help shape these complicated processes of transition and innovation.

Private enterprise is at a crossroads in deciding to take the lead to enter this new phase on its own account or to wait and expect governments to prescribe the conditions for future production. If private enterprise goes proactively ahead it may demand that government create the proper conditions for sustainable enterprise, for example in the necessary social and economic conditions for this process of transition. Education levels need to be improved and support is needed for the development of knowledge, and of 'macro' technology systems for sustainable energy use, sustainable transportation systems and infrastructures, and sustainable land use to encourage integration. Also, business will expect the government to co-finance such investment projects and to cover financial risks that exceed normal business risks. And private enterprise will expect the government to facilitate a societal debate that leads to clear objectives and timeframes for achieving sustainable management of natural capital, both nationally and internationally.

Towards new business strategies for sustainability

Recent research on progress towards sustainable business strategies in a number of important Netherlands' companies shows that many larger enterprises experience great difficulty in making this next move towards sustainability (VROM 2001b). This research identifies four major impediments for progress. First, relatively short time horizons for major investment decisions block sight of the major ecological and economic changes that influence the potential for renewal of the enterprise. Second, most companies overestimate the importance of realised efforts on environmental improvement so far. They focus on the improvement of environmental quality of production process, and hardly touch upon improved environmental conditions in the supply chain. Product innovation to realise resource productivity remains another rather new issue to most enterprises. Third, internal management structures are not geared towards the identification of opportunities for ecological modernisation. Lastly, enterprises appear to have insufficient knowledge of the drivers for ecological change of important societal organisations from NGOs, consumer organisations, pension funds or labour unions.

This analysis leads to four recommendations to improve the internal strategy development of enterprises:

1 systematic investigation of the ecological and business horizon of the firm and identification of relevant discontinuities in both areas;
2 systematic charting of regular business relations and stakeholders of the firm, and also systematic identification of potential new players and stakeholders in the supply and technology chains;
3 systematic strategic investigation of sources of potential value creation, allowing attention not only for eco-efficiency improvements and cost savings, but also for the potential development of

ecologically and economically superior products and purely 'green' products;

4   development of internal organisation structures that allow the full integration of the above-mentioned systematic investigations at all levels and in all sections of the company.

An analysis of progress towards these stages of sustainability in 11 prominent Dutch companies showed that a number of important conditions for the internal organisation of enterprises need to be met (see Chapter 5). Key to this process is support from the board and sponsorship from the chief executive officer. These elements appear essential for adequate internal processes of ecological modernisation. Also, it appears necessary to upgrade environmental work in the company beyond the responsibility of the environmental officers. Cross-functional teams from all parts of the organisation appear necessary for progress towards sustainability. A next important internal organisational change is the integrated collection and reporting of economic, social and ecological data. Finally, the development of long-term objectives is needed to organise a strategic reorientation of the firm.

In the next stages of sustainable development, environmental business strategy will need to go beyond risk reduction and cost cutting. Sustainability requires a reorientation towards tomorrow's technologies and markets. William McDonough and Michael Braungart, American and German specialists in this field, call for the design of new criteria for business investment strategies and recommend the following steps to gradually lead the company to become a sustainable enterprise (Braungart and McDonough 2000: 55).

1   *Signal your intention:* Commit to the new paradigm of the sustainable enterprise; do not just improve the old model but signal a change in the framework itself. Radiate that in due time you are going to make solar-based products. It may be clear that good design is founded on healthy principles all the way. Do not accept partial solutions or substitution of one evil for another.

2   *Enrich the investment criteria:* Add new criteria on required inherent ecological soundness of new products and production technologies to the traditional investment criteria.

3   *Innovate:* Thrive and do not simply survive. Recognise that innovation occurs within niches for a competitive edge. Recognise the opportunities of new markets, especially in emerging and poor economies. What can your company do to begin a new industrial

revolution to feed, house and warm 10 billion people in a social and ecological equitable way?

4   *Rematerialise:* Rather than simply working to make a product less harmful, make a product with no harmful substances that can be safely recycled.

5   *Accrue wealth:* Become wealthier in natural and industrial materials. Bring them out of the cradle-to-grave system and support the development of a cradle-to-cradle system. Circulate materials for industry. They are worth billions of dollars.

6   *No regulations, but good economics, good sense and good fun:* Fun in the sense that one could use the product free of guilt because it was designed to be inherently sustainable.

The process of transition is a complicated one. Present interests cannot be disconnected from future prospects. Going through transition stages of predevelopment of new products and new processes, through a stage towards increased market penetration, is a slow process. Transition management at the firm level requires a vision that includes both a long-term target area, as well as short-term gains with a focus on how to move from today's wastes and emissions to tomorrow's sustainable products, processes and markets. New coalitions need to be formed, both internally and externally, in the product chain, in the technology chain and with governments and NGOs.

A summary program for governments and enterprises for the transition to the sustainable enterprise

A program to achieve inherent modes of sustainable enterprise where full account is given to both qualitative and volume aspects of the management of natural capital, in the broad context of social, economic and ecological concerns, involves the following:

1   *Sustainable energy supply is the first key to sustainable development.* Private enterprise in collaboration with governments needs to accelerate the development of infrastructure and technology for sustainable energy. Present objectives for the development of sustainable energy supply appear too unambitious to achieve the present obligations of the Kyoto Protocol and to have a timely transition to a sustainable energy economy.

2   *Sustainable land use is the second key to sustainable development.* Enterprises should engage in the development of new alliances for

the timely creation of sustainable infrastructures for transportation, dwellings and industrial sites. Governments should facilitate such processes of transition and should provide financial support to take away above-level economic risks. Private enterprise, banks and pension funds in collaboration with governments must generate venture capital for the development of these sustainable infrastructures.

3   *Private enterprise should take the lead in determining long-term objectives* for the restoration of environmental quality, and for the preservation of stocks of biodiversity and nature. It should set its own targets for the radical reduction of the use of fossil fuels, for dematerialising production, for total recycling of waste products, and for the strengthening social infrastructures.

4   *Government and private enterprise should work on the broadening of fiscal regimes* to incorporate and reflect true environmental costs to society. Intensification of land-use planning directions to spare scarce land and nature resources, and the introduction of new instruments such as, for example, tradable emission rights to limit the use of scarce minerals and of fossil fuels will be necessary.

5   *Governments should provide venture capital and export credit guarantees* to companies involved in the development and transition of new technologies to Eastern European countries and to the Third World.

6   *The example role of the government is to be strengthened* by intensification of government procurement policies to the exclusive purchase of sustainable products.

7   *Governments should demand that private enterprise enhance transparency* of its practices through statutory obligations for measuring and reporting on relevant environmental aspects of its operations and of its social conduct. Codes of conduct should become compulsory for companies operating in Eastern Europe and in Third-World countries.

Expanding the ecological policy arena not only to include economic interests but to engage all relevant social and economic cross-sectoral interests is an important direction in which to move. This requires new forms and forums to ensure the participation of the broadest possible array of stakeholders for the design of solutions that challenge all interests involved. In the debate on shaping the sustainable enterprise there are no easy answers and it concerns a complicated search for modernisation.

5 Management strategies for sustainable businesses[1]

Business appears to be entering a stage marked by a new series of developing sustainability issues, and a widening array of stakeholders. While earlier stages focused on environmental quality protection, and were handled within the company itself, this new stage of sustainable entrepreneurship differs in complexity and orientation (Kolk and Mauser 2002: 14; see also Chapter 4). Now, sustainable entrepreneurship addresses issues of preservation of resource stocks of biodiversity, nature, energy, water and minerals. The integration of ecological and social demands has raised national and international sustainability issues related to community development, human rights, human resources, trade regulations and health and safety. Thus, this stage of sustainable entrepreneurship requires externally oriented approaches to adequately handle the strategic management of the increasingly complex processes involving a growing number of stakeholder groups (Clarke and Roome 1999: 296).

These new demands and associated consequences for business strategy and organisation received attention in the literature (Roome 1998; Welford 1998; Boons and Berends 2001). Although authors link research on sustainable strategies to regular business management literature, this link needs further exploration. Generally speaking, the literature is based on an implicit notion that sustainable strategies and organisation are qualitatively different from regular management procedures. Modern views of business administration deal with many of the issues that are central to sustainability. Business management theories of 'stakeholder approaches' and 'the knowledge-based firm' are connected to the organisational questions of sustainable entrepreneurship; 'resource-based' theories deal with the strategic management of resources and capabilities.

In this chapter the application of insights of business management theory in developing a systematic perspective on sustainable business is reviewed. It brings a new perspective on sustainable entrepreneurship.

An investigation of this development in 11 multinationals in the Netherlands adds empirical insight to the theoretical analysis of business administration literature. The companies of this empirical survey were selected because of their reputation on advanced policies of environmental management and their attempts to broaden the focus to sustainable entrepreneurship. The investigation focused on identifying the obstacles to the process of change, and determining recommendations to enhance the process. 'Stakeholder theory' and 'resource-based theory' of business management served as the theoretical framework for analysis.

The research was launched in 2001, and a comprehensive report was published in Dutch, presenting a concise analysis of empirical material collected at the following companies: Heineken, Coca Cola, Suikerunie, Nutreco, Van Melle, Akzo Nobel, DSM, Ytong, ING-bank, Rabobank and Nuon.[2] Two questions guided the research:

1   Are companies entering a new management stage in which new sustainability issues dominate the agenda involving a wider array of stakeholders?
2   How are companies managing the strategic process of adapting their internal resources to these new demands of the growing number of stakeholders?

A model was developed to support the analysis of the advancement of firms in the management of sustainability in three stages (Keijzers *et al.* 2002: 37):

1   sanitation (clean-up efforts of enterprises)
2   adequate environmental management (by pollution prevention and eco-efficiency of production)
3   integration (of all ecological and social issues into all business decisions).

Regarding the contents of sustainability issues, the stage of integration is characterised by technological innovations and transitions towards new technology systems, and by the greater attention to national and international social issues (Welford 1998: 243).

Before reporting the findings, insights from the business management theories applied as a theoretic framework of analysis of the strategic management of sustainability were reviewed. This summary included the major lines of reasoning and implications of the 'stakeholder theory' and of the 'resource-based theories' related to the sustainability agenda.

Conclusions and recommendations for enterprises in transition to integrated sustainability approaches in business strategies were also identified.

A new agenda for sustainable business strategies: selected insights from business management theory

An important aspect of sustainable business strategy is the relationship with stakeholders. A sustainable strategy deals with the position of a firm within society. Rather than seeing society as an abstract entity with driving forces and trends, the stakeholder approach operationalises society as a set of actors who are influenced by, or can influence, the firm. Addressing the position of the firm in society then becomes a matter of strategically handling the relationship with these actors, the stakeholders.

Stakeholder approaches are not unique to the debates on sustainability. The management literature deals with this issue as early as Ansoff's standard work on strategy that considered the limits of the firm to be determined by the demands of its stakeholders (Ansoff 1965). With the work of Freeman (1984), stakeholder management became an accepted term in the literature, and found its way into practice. As such, stakeholder management centres on the following questions (Carrol and Bucholtz 2002):

What stakeholders need to be dealt with?

Freeman defined stakeholders as all those who can influence the objectives of the firm, or are influenced by the firm, in attaining their own objectives. The set of actors identified is extensive, and includes consumers and suppliers, employees, shareholders, environmentalist groups, trade unions, local communities and governmental bodies.

Thus, dealing with stakeholders is a matter of selecting the stakeholders that really matter. Mitchell *et al.* argue that there are three criteria used for this selection process (Mitchell *et al.* 1997: 853). First, the *power* a stakeholder has over the firm. Power is related to dependency, and centers on the question of how much the firm needs the resources supplied by that stakeholder only. The resources can be material (like raw materials) but can also be immaterial, such as knowledge. A second variable is *legitimacy*. This is about legitimate claims of a stakeholder on the firm. Governmental bodies are important in this respect, because they have the legitimacy to develop rules for firms. A final variable is *urgency*: the claims of stakeholders can differ with respect to the urgency of a response of the firm. Much of the literature on stakeholder approaches deals with the bilateral relation between the firm and each of its stakeholders. Rowley has drawn attention to the fact that stakeholders may have connections, and that the firm operates in a network of stakeholders (Rowley 1997: 887). This implies that a stakeholder may not be crucial given the variables of legitimacy, power or urgency, but it still should be selected because it influences other stakeholders that are important to the firm. An example of this would be the local community of a crucial supplier of the firm.

What form should the relationship with a stakeholder take?

In the literature on sustainability, the relation with stakeholders is often coined as 'dialogue'. Although this is an important variant, it is not the only type of relationship that can exist between a firm and one or more stakeholders. Interaction possibilities range from simple sharing of information to full strategic partnerships or outright competition. Also, 'negative' interactions such as strikes and legal procedures should be included.

How should stakeholder management be linked to internal processes?

The management of stakeholders should be connected to the internal process of the firm. Members of the firm continuously interact with representatives of stakeholder organisations. Stakeholder approaches also deal with the way in which these interactions are co-ordinated internally, and linked to operational processes as well as the formulation of strategies. This is a crucial element, further explored in the next section.

Much of the literature on stakeholder theory implicitly deals with managing the status quo in an efficient way. Relevant stakeholders need to be detected and dealt with in such a way that their legitimate claims are acknowledged and the continuity of the firm is secured. This leads to the following critical questions:

- How should a firm deal with stakeholders in terms of innovative activities (rather than consolidating the status quo)?
- What if the firm's activities are inherently unsustainable, and sustainability is thus best served by discontinuation of these activities, or even of the firm as it currently exists?

An approach that can deal with such questions is one based on the work of Boons and Berends (2001), Roome (2001) and Chisholm (1998). It starts with the idea that any firm is part of a socio-technical system, which has its own dynamics and life cycle. In the course of time, the system evolves from a new venture to a growing production and consumption system where routines become engrained and relations institutionalised, and consequently innovations aim at improving efficiency rather than dealing with the fundamentals on which the system is based. This has several implications for sustainability, but in this context, the idea that stakeholder management for the sustainable firm should somehow start from this perspective of being part of a socio-technical system is the focus. Boons and Berends imply that the firm needs to deal with its stakeholders in terms of being a part of the total system, and sustainable development of the system as a major goal (Boons and Berends 2001).

This is in fact close to the idea of Rowley when he writes about the network of stakeholders. Depending on the density of the network, and the centrality of the firm in this network, the firm should develop its strategy towards stakeholders. If the firm has a central position, such as being one of the major producers in a production and consumption system, it can take a leading role in the sustainable development of the system. On the other hand, if the firm is a small part of such a system it can only take part in system-wide efforts that are initiated by others.

Insights from network management and collective learning can help in making this perspective work. Checkland (1981) developed a general outline of a process in which system actors work together to formulate system goals, and subsequently develop projects in which these goals are achieved. It can be seen as a continuous learning cycle for the whole system. The cycle has a phase of *reflection* in which ambitions are formulated and translated into demands for the system as a whole. This leads into a phase of *action*, where system demands are operationalised into projects that are implemented by sets of system actors.

After assessing the results of these projects, the phase of reflection can be entered again to reassess ambitions as well as the question of the appropriate system boundary. Clarke and Roome (1999) developed a similar idea about strategies for firms that are involved in what they call an *action-learning network*. Research testing the developments with respect to these assumptions on action-learning networks, and continuous learning cycles of stakeholder engagement of the investigated firms, is included in the next section. The focus is on the implications for strategic management theory as analysed in 'resource-based' theories.

While stakeholder theory advises that firms continuously consider and manage the changing needs of stakeholders, 'resource-based theory' stresses the need for enterprises to maintain a flexible internal organisational architecture able to adapt to these changing needs (Barney and Arikan 2001: 124). Hence, adjusting business strategies to the new demands of ecological and socioeconomic sustainability not only requires adequate stakeholder approaches to understand changes arising from sustainability; proper analysis is also required to test the adaptability of a firm's internal resources and capabilities to adjust to these changing needs. Indeed, it appears that sustainability is very demanding in terms of innovative capacity and of adaptability of the firm. 'Resource-based' views provide a strong framework to structure the analysis of the strengths and weaknesses of a firm's internal resources and capabilities with respect to present and potential competitive advantages.

Building on Ricardian theory of rent and on Penrosian business growth economics, the 'resource-based theory' is founded in two basic assumptions (Barney 2002: 155). First, there is an assumption of resource heterogeneity of competing firms, implying that different firms possess different bundles of resources that explain their comparative advantages in markets. Second, the assumption of resource immobility implies that the competitive advantage of a firm is also based on the firm's possession and exploitation of *distinctive* resources and capabilities.

Kay summarises the main elements of the 'resource-based theory' (Kay 1996: 34):

- firms are essentially collections of capabilities and the effectiveness of a firm depends on the match between these capabilities and the market it serves;
- the growth and appropriate boundaries of a firm are limited by its capabilities;
- some capabilities can be purchased or created and are available to all firms;
- others are irreproducible, or reproducible only with substantial difficulty, by other firms, and it is on these *distinctive* resources and capabilities that competitive advantage depends;
- such capabilities are generally irreproducible because they are a product of the history of the firm.

Value-chain analysis of a firm may support the strategic analysis of the identification of its *distinctive* resources and capabilities (Barney 2002: 160). Analysis of a firm's strategic strengths and weaknesses, according to 'resource-based' views, requires assessment of the value and adaptability of the firm's resources and capabilities in all the parts of the value chain with respect to the ability to respond to threats and opportunities from business surroundings. Kay emphasises the necessity of a strategic audit to build adequate business strategies (Barney 2002: 163). Such audits address questions such as:

- What are the firm's distinctive capabilities (trust, quality of service, innovative capacity, adaptability of internal architecture, information capabilities and so forth)?
- Are the markets in which the company operates markets where distinctive capabilities add value?
- Are there other markets the firm is not yet in, where it might enjoy competitive advantage (the question of identification of new opportunities in present or new markets)?
- How can competitive advantage be sustained and appropriated (the question of analysis of potential threats of new entries, potential substitutes, suppliers and customers)?

Business strategies for sustainability differ from general business strategies in that they try to react to or exploit changing market and regulatory demands that enhance sustainable conditions for ecological preservation and social equity. These issues of sustainability appear very intensive on the strategic management of the firm. The assessment of a firm's capability to direct and adjust its distinctive resources to the changing demands on sustainability in the markets it is operating in, or it plans to start operations in, requires analyses as proposed in the strategic audit to build adequate business strategies.

An analysis of business strategies in the 11 companies in the Netherlands focused on changes at three levels:

1 adjustment of internal resources and capabilities
2 development of processes to identify changing external stakeholder demands
3 organisational changes to relate new external information on sustainability requirements to the internal architecture of the firm.

Sustainable development demands extensive direct and intermediate changes and innovations of products and markets. These requirements may render threats and opportunities to enterprises. Companies that are able to understand the signals of sustainability from changing sets of stakeholder groups, and that are equipped to adjust their resources to meet the new demands, are best able to make the transition to sustainable entrepreneurship, i.e. the third stage of integrated strategic management and exploitation of potentials and threats related to sustainable development. Kay states this as, 'The successful firm is one which creates a *distinctive* character in these relationships and which operates in an environment which maximizes the value of that *distinctiveness*' (Kay 1996: 37).

These considerations indicate that the strategic management of the successful sustainable enterprise simultaneously demands the highest performance in terms of innovation of products, production processes, market-reorientation and stakeholder engagement by the firm. This requires the full use of business management strategies.

Summary of research findings

Using the theoretical insights discussed above, the main findings of empirical research are summarised.

The 11 companies that were investigated achieved what is identified in the introductory section as 'stage two' of adequate environmental management of business operations. All enterprises appear to be approaching 'stage three', the integration of the broader aspects of sustainability in their business strategies and practices. The research completed indicates that the 'stage two' environmental management procedures of linking environmental aspects to general managerial procedures of the firm relates to substantial improvements in environmental performance. These improvements have been realised through formalised *internal* organisational routines that systematically take aspects of environmental protection into account. All companies aligned their internal *resources and capabilities* to handle the demands of adequate environmental management.

Companies practised processes of *internal* organisational change to incorporate environmental protection issues in all sectors of their enterprise, ranging from purchase, production, logistics, marketing and sales. This learning process was a challenge, and integration of environmental management in the *internal* organisation met with resistance. In the situation where traditional responsibilities need to be shared, this unavoidably appeared to require nothing less than cultural change processes within the enterprise. In some enterprises these organisational learning processes were initiated and guided by the top management. In others, the processes gradually developed from the bottom up. In line with resource-based theory, although companies use identical labels such as 'quality control' and 'environmental management system', each company has its own unique way of organising these activities. This holds also for the process of change. In one instance, a company tried a bottom-up approach as advocated by consultants, only to find out that a top-down approach better suited the corporate culture.

In the developing the 'third stage' of integration, traditional environmental quality protection issues, as well as the new sustainability issues of preservation of resources stocks and of the holistic social and ecological perspectives, becomes structurally integrated into the operational and strategic management of the firm. Most companies in the research were aware of the importance of these upcoming issues of sustainability. Yet many enterprises experienced great difficulty in incorporating them into organisational routines, and appeared to find it complex to determine new attitudes towards new stakeholder groups. The companies were aware of the potential business economics threats and opportunities connected to the sustainability issues of the stage of integration, and of the need to adjust their *internal resources and capabilities* to these new requirements.

All companies participating in the research have applied strategic management procedures for the identification of new market opportunities related to the changing conditions of sustainability. Some companies started specific programs for the promotion of innovation through product stewardship. Others are adding issues of sustainability to existing regular strategic routines and audits for the identification of business opportunities. Some enterprises are designing new search efforts in and beyond the company to identify options for technological renewal and innovation in view of arising demands of sustainability. And most companies are right in the middle of a search process to find strategic management routines to adjust these changing external conditions. The procedures adopted appear to relate to regular approaches of strategic management.

The enterprises also expressed difficulty in determining appropriate and clear short- and intermediate-term goals for sustainable strategies. This was especially the case in determining business objectives and strategies for the introduction of new technology. Incremental technology changes appear to dominate the attention over more radical systems changes that are deemed necessary for transitions toward sustainable production processes in, for instance, energy, chemicals and food production. The economic risks of 'own' corporate technology development were shown to be economically riskier over time, with most companies reporting that the larger parts of research and development efforts were reduced or eliminated. All companies claimed the necessity for joint societal and shared company efforts for the transition to new technology systems and infrastructures. Even the largest international corporations showed remarkable dependent positions.

Although the companies stated an awareness of the need for 'stakeholder dialogue', they experienced difficulties in exactly this field of technological renewal to organise a meaningful interaction with stakeholders, and to connect it to the internal process.

Strategic management demands a high degree of internal adaptability of *resources and capabilities* to the new external demands. As such, companies continually build on internal resources and capabilities through new acquisitions, disposals, mergers and otherwise rearranged company interests. Business-based economic decisions for the better strategic positioning of the enterprise caused these realignments. Often, however, negative and positive consequences for the sustainability position of the company were experienced. Some companies reported, for instance, that through new acquisitions they had improved the corporate position for innovative technological development of production processes and product development, or improved environmental control of the supply chain. From a perspective of enhanced sustainable entrepreneurship, the drawback of the processes of continuous mergers points to a trend towards aversion of financial risks, thus limiting the options for investment in innovations with a focus on long-term continuity and sustainability.

Two enterprises that were investigated in the chemical sector are examples of remarkable changes in the portfolio composition. Both companies made the strategic business decision to move from basic chemicals production to chemicals and pharmaceuticals higher up in the value chain, characterised by higher value-added levels, and more advanced levels of sustainability qualities. These firms also sought acquisitions to advance sustainable technology opportunities, and to enhance the adaptability of their *resources and capabilities* to the changing needs of sustainability. The same applied to the energy company in the research. The banks and the enterprises in the food production sector limited their sustainable strategy activities to the networks of the supply chain and the local surroundings, only partially engaging in the approaches to holistic technological renewal of the production and consumption systems they are part of.

It is thus useful to distinguish the three levels of stakeholder environment of the firm:

1   the local environment
2   the product chain
3   the production and consumption system.

At the first level, firms (i.e. their various production and administrative facilities) are situated in locations where they are increasingly confronted with demands from the local community as well as the surrounding firms. The companies included in the research are confronted with development and collaboration in eco-industrial parks. As a consequence, the firms need to consider building links with other firms to exchange waste streams, share utilities or develop joint logistics and distribution systems, and engage in efforts to develop sustainable energy infrastructure. This poses problems of increased dependency. In addition, as many production facilities are part of larger, and often multinational, legal entities, the companies experience increased pressure to focus on production efficiency, limiting room for innovative solutions at the local levels. Despite these extra pressures there was an increased willingness to participate or even to initiate such locally bounded industrial ecosystems. Although these actions to start collaboration at the level of the local environment are considered to be at the first level of the collective learning processes, they appear to provide a basis for more radical innovations.

At the second level of the product chain, most firms initiated supply chain management, inclusive of environmental issues, and sometimes integrated with quality and health and safety issues. Organisational changes mostly pertained to collaborative efforts to integrate environmental controls and environmental product care in the enterprises linked in the network of the supply chain, often formalised in systems of strategic alliances with preferred suppliers and customers. The frontrunners amongst the investigated companies, in terms of advanced sustainability attention, made obvious progress with processes of integration of environmental concerns in the management of the supply and technology chains. These efforts are important steps towards sustainable entrepreneurship, yet in itself supply chain management does not need to contribute to sustainability. In fact, it can also be used simply as a power strategy to bind suppliers to the firm and make them more dependent and controllable. One of the firms researched developed an information system for its supply chain that served the dual purpose of binding suppliers as well as making it possible to track the quality of the products, and thus to develop a differentiated product palette including more sustainable products.

Handling external relations at the third level of total product and consumption systems, of which enterprises are part, is the most encompassing process change and firms seem hesitant to deal with it in a systematic way. Recent Dutch national environmental policy programs proclaim holistic transitions towards sustainability in such systems as their main goal (VROM 2001a). Firms are encouraged to participate in 'transition programs' of technology and socio-technological systems. They are further urged to take part in the collective learning cycles of *action-learning networks* around the development of systems such as sustainable infrastructures for transport and energy. With few exceptions, firms find these goals of sustainable development too abstract and, although they understand the importance, their focus seems to be on a much shorter term. Factors such as the attention for shareholder value and account-ability of business units reinforce this short-term perspective. The longer-term focus for sustainability and economic continuity of the firm seems at best competing with this short-term focus. Most investigated companies did not seem ready for the necessary fundamental systems change of open stakeholder involvement. It appears complicated to engage in new alliances in production and technology chains to start fundamental processes of technological transition towards sustainable energy, chemical, transport and food production.

In the investigation of stakeholder approaches, a smaller number of companies did engage in open processes of 'stakeholder dialogue' aimed at learning from external stakeholders in order to adjust internal resources to the new demands. They report that the open and proactive learning process of stakeholder dialogue requires open agendas and a willingness on all sides to interactively learn in the process. This also requires lasting processes of building of trust, and the continuous development of learning capabilities both on the part of the enterprises and the stakeholder organisations. Such processes appear to develop only slowly in the firms studied. Making the connection between the external stakeholder dialogue and internal processes is also a major problem for most companies.

At the brink of 'stage three', Dutch industry seems to show resistance to broadening its strategic scope towards sustainability. The enterprises often explained this reluctance from the true fact that enormous environmental progress had been achieved so far. Also, they argued that limitations to progress are due to the slower processes in competing industries in other countries. Enterprises also claimed that the great uncertainties and economic risks involved in the introduction of new technologies kept them from fundamental strategic changes.

Summary of recommendations: organising the next stage of sustainable entrepreneurship

The design of new strategic management procedures for the third stage of sustainable entrepreneurship is based on good business theories. As demonstrated by a theoretical as well as empirical perspective, much can be learned from 'general' prescriptive theories of management, since they address issues that are vital to sustainable business. Successful business strategies require good understanding of and collaboration with external stakeholders, as well as flexibility of the internal organisation of the firm's resources and capabilities. The next stages of sustainable entrepreneurship have to deal with the following three areas of change:

1   managing the flexibility of the internal organisation through the maintenance of environmental management tools and the application of strategic instruments to incorporate issues of sustainability in strategy and investment decisions;
2   managing change in the supply and technology chains;
3   enhancing stakeholder approaches by expanding to engage all stakeholders in the understanding of the new sustainability demands, and to learn from these relations about the design of adequate responses.

Further investigation leads to the following recommendations:

1   To facilitate the required processes of learning and of cultural change of the internal organisation, it is necessary to integrate environmental and social issues of sustainability in *all* business processes, at *all* levels, and in *all* divisions of the organisation. Commitment for change can only be gained when staff learn about their importance. In some business cultures the first moves towards sustainability need to come from the top; in others the top must first be convinced by actions from the bottom up. The process demands the application of regular environmental management tools, as well as regular management instruments, for organisational change. As evidenced by stakeholder theory, in such collective learning processes actors within the firm work together internally as well as with actors in the related external networks in the production and consumption system as a whole. In these continuous and iterative learning cycles the ambitions are jointly formulated and translated into concrete projects for the enterprise and its related networks. Supportive actions for internal change processes for *organisational action-learning* may be:

1.1 start up of environmental pilots in *all* organisational units to test potential projects of sustainability for business opportunities;

1.2 develop *cross-functional* project teams and workshops to identify business opportunities that arise from sustainability, and to identify potential threats from strategies of business-as-usual;

1.3 develop relevant *business cases* (of challenging integrated business and environment opportunities) for renewal to a sustainable business;

1.4 use such *business cases* to gain support from the top;

1.5 introduce aspects of sustainability in training programs and in *human resource management* in general;

1.6 introduce environmental and social audits and reports, and start procedures to integrate those with financial reports for the support of learning processes.

2 Sustainable business strategies often require fundamental changes rather than incremental changes of operations. Change will only materialise in the organisation when the firm is visibly and whole-heartedly committed to the paradigm of sustainability. The internal organisation of strategic decision-making processes needs to be adjusted for the high-risk levels attached to these potentially fundamental changes. To support investment decisions and business redirections, the firm should conduct *strategic audits* to identify and to determine its *distinctive* resources and capabilities. The 'resource-based theory' emphasises the necessity to assess the value of the firm's resources and capabilities, and of its ability to respond to threats and opportunities from its business surroundings. It is necessary to establish whether the markets in which the company operates are markets in which its *distinctive* capabilities add value, and continue to do so. Equally necessary is answering questions on the identification of new opportunities in present or new markets. To facilitate sustainable investment decisions it is necessary to broaden the set of traditional investment criteria by including criteria on the ecological and social implications of potential investment projects. Supportive actions for the adjustment of these strategy development processes might be:

2.1 explore systematically potentially new sources of value creation for the firm, by constantly executing strategic checks on potentials for investments from the integrated perspective of sustainability, and identify options for:

2.1.1 cost reductions

2.1.2 product differentiation

2.1.3 product/market differentiation;

2.2 explore systematically the potentials for new players in present and potential supply chain and technology chains;

2.3 explore systematically the vulnerability of the firm's present resources and capabilities with respect to their adaptability to new market demands;

2.4 explore systematically the horizons for new business and for new environmental demands, and identify potential discontinuities in either area, which may call for natural moments for changes in sustainable business strategy.

3 Transition to the sustainable business implies the need to participate in supply chains in which companies strive for sustainable production. The development of *action-learning networks* demands intensified efforts of collaboration in stakeholder networks of the supply and technology chains. Improved transparency of activities in the chain is necessary to elicit potential economic and ecological advantages of sustainable approaches. Also, the network of the supply chain itself, and of connecting networks, needs to be adequately managed to enhance joint processes of organisational learning and joint sharing of responsibilities to address the new demands of sustainable products and production processes. The application of information and communications technology enhances knowledge and vulnerability of and within the supply chain. This aspect requires considerate management in the arising stage of sustainable entrepreneurship. Supportive activities to exploit the opportunities for more sustainable supply chains are:

3.1 set up joint supply chain workshops to identify opportunities and threats deriving from sustainable development, and to enhance network operations and transparency in the chain;

3.2 start up joint programs for integrated chain information and control, product care and product stewardship in order to organise the integration of regular supply chain management activities with specific issues of sustainability;

3.3 develop joint long-term objectives for sustainable business in the supply chain and start joint public/private investigations into improvements to ensure sustainable infrastructural amenities for supplies of energy, water, transport and waste disposal facilities;

3.4 organise strategic business partnerships in the supply chain to handle joint interests with national and European governments for the continuation of, or development of, supportive economic regulations and structures to ensure long-term continuity of conditions enhancing sustainable production in the supply chain.

4   Sustainable business strategies require full understanding of interests of stakeholders, and the firm's ability to engage in dialogue and joint learning processes with the changing and widening array of stakeholders. Enterprises should be open and willing to learn from interactive stakeholder approaches at the levels of the direct physical and social surroundings of the firm, of the supply and technology chains, and of the total production and consumption systems, including the private and public firms providing and developing infrastructural services. Enterprises should engage in strategic alliances for the accelerated development of sustainable infrastructures for energy, transport and communication, and for the development of sustainable spatial plans at local and regional levels. Based on the literature and findings, recommendations point to firms developing an approach to stakeholders that takes the production and consumption system of which they are a part of as a starting point. In doing so, the focus should be on developing and maintaining a collective learning cycle in this system that can make progressive steps towards sustainable development. This serves the system as a whole as well as the individual firm. Connecting internal processes to this collective learning cycle is vital. In that way, the firm's research and development and strategic management are aligned with the evolution of the production and consumption system as a whole.

Implementing these recommendations is a challenge, especially where the link is made to the production and consumption system of which individual firms are part. But as a recent European Union (EU) study concluded: although much has been achieved in terms of improving environmental performance, 'the European system of production is not sustainable' (EU 2001: xi). This can only be achieved by a change effort in which firms, governmental agencies and societal actors take production and consumption systems, rather than their individual activities, as the focus for change. The above recommendations serve as guidance for companies to take steps to be involved in this major effort.

6 Plotting sustainable directions for business

An evolving stakeholder approach in seven multinationals

Collaborative stakeholder approaches

Increasingly, ecological and social demands from a growing number of stakeholders add to the traditional economic and technical demands on a company's products, services and production processes. Scientific evidence is more and more showing the importance of a stakeholder approach in incorporating these evolving demands into business strategies (Wheeler and Sillanpaa 1997; Harrison and St John 1998; Collins and Porras 1998; Svendsen 1998; Clarke and Roome 1999; Harrison and Freeman 1999; Freeman and McVea 2001; World Business Council for Sustainable Development [WBCSD] 2002; Waddock 2002).

For the development of corporate social responsibility (CR) strategies as such, and for the development of business strategies in general, it is important for companies to engage with stakeholders and learn about CR issues. Integrating this stakeholder approach into organisational structures and operational mechanisms is the new challenge. An empirical study, based on stakeholder theory, of the stakeholder approach for CR strategy development in seven multinational corporations in the United Kingdom (UK) and the Netherlands (Shell, Heineken, Diageo, Unilever, Ahold, Numico, ING-bank) provides learning points.[1]

It appears from this empirical research that the long-term value drivers for CR business strategies (to enhance strategies for continuity of the company) are quite different from the short-term value drivers (for reputation management); these differences between short-term and long-term interests require a different stakeholder approach.

Short-term interests, e.g. shareholders wanting higher profits, employees wanting a pay rise, surrounding communities wanting improved environmental protection levels, or human rights organisations wanting better labour conditions, all require intensive deliberation with the related stakeholder groups. It is of great importance to the company to be actively informed about these demands to establish its own position and to determine a strategy. *The common denominator of all these short-term stakeholder interests is that they can be identified, quantified and qualified.* The company can subsequently assess its position and make strategic decisions to balance and reconcile the conflicting interests of the various stakeholder groups. Or it may decide not to, and accept the consequences of the confrontation with one or more of its stakeholders.

Short-term *stakeholder management* is radically different from stakeholder approaches to long-term stakeholder interests, which focus on sustainable development of society and on continuity of the company. *Long-term stakeholder interests share the common aspect that although the direction of change towards sustainability can be established, the objectives for sustainability in general, or for the company's long-term success, remain obscure.* The exact meaning and importance of these objectives needs to develop in societal processes, balancing ecological, social and ecological demands, and gauging future economic and technological opportunities (see also Chapter 3). The number of stakeholders constantly widens. Business strategies incorporating the stakeholder demands on issues of sustainability and CR are growing in importance. The rapid changes in industrialised countries with respect to sustainable production practices, and the increasing need for companies to extend to growing markets in developing countries, presents businesses with a whole range of new management issues and an increasing number of stakeholders. Continuity of the company in industrialised markets demands broader stakeholder relationships, which must consider such new issues as technology and infrastructure development for the sustainable production of energy, transport, chemicals, food and nature conservation. In addition, capitalising on the tremendous potential for market growth in countries in transition and in the Third World requires equally intensive strategy considerations (Hart 1997). The new stakeholder approach in these countries calls for even more complicated processes (Prahalad and Hart 2002: 54).

The central concern of the company should be to understand its stakeholders, and to continue satisfying stakeholder objectives in order to create the right conditions for continuity (Freeman and McVea 2001: 193). Companies will at least want to ensure adequate lines of production, yet it is equally important to achieve joint social, ecological and economic conditions, as well as technical infrastructures, for future production. CR business strategies aim to achieve these essential conditions for long-term continuity, and stakeholder approaches seem crucial to determine the related requirements. Enduring and successful companies maintain a robust core ideology aimed at serving and achieving the objectives of its stakeholders (Collins and Porras 1998). The minimum requirement for long-term continuity of the company is proper knowledge of the 'limitations' set by the long-term demands of stakeholders, and by the willingness and ability to translate these 'limitations' in interaction and collaboration with the stakeholders. As a result, there is a critical role for shared values between companies and stakeholders. To visionary companies, profitability is not a primary business objective, but a means of achieving the broader array of objectives and purposes set out in the core ideology.

Summary of empirical study findings

In the autumn of 2001, research on the stakeholder approach of seven multinational companies with respect to the development of their CR business strategy was conducted. In this research, identifying the important value drivers for CR strategies, as well as essential supportive internal and external organisational mechanisms, was the focus.

The companies involved are based in the UK and the Netherlands: Shell, ING, Unilever, Ahold, Diageo, Heineken and Numico.[2] The relevant publicly available documents (company codes of conduct, operational CR guidelines and audit reports) and the websites of these companies with respect to their stakeholder approach and CR policy were analysed.[3] Also, semi-structured interviews with representatives from these companies, mostly high-level staff responsible for public affairs, were conducted. These interviews, which took about two to three hours each, were professionally documented and checked for accuracy by the interviewees.

The companies that were researched all operate business units in many countries around the globe. They are active in industrialised as well as developing countries, and have to face a wide diversity of cultural, political and socioeconomic conditions. All companies carry A-brand products and services. The combination of these conditions makes these companies rather vulnerable to stakeholder demands on social and ecological responsibilities. These conditions also seem to provide opportunities for stakeholder approaches aiming to develop business strategies for long-term continuity.

All companies in the research formulated a set of business principles expressing values on CR issues. Most of them had put operational documents in place, laying out guidelines for management and employees on CR practices. Three companies had issued extensive external reports on their CR program. In no case did the enterprises address all the relevant CR issues; rather, most companies focused on a relatively limited set of topics. External pressures appeared important in the selection of priority topics, as limited organisational capacity in all companies called for priority setting and phasing of the CR program. A wider range of topics is likely to involve additional organisational efforts to adequately engage internal and external stakeholders. Only a small number of companies have gone through a process addressing most of the relevant issues. All companies appear to struggle with these aspects of priority setting with respect to the demands of stakeholders. They need to react to *immediate demands of stakeholders*, and attempt to allow sufficient time for the development of CR policies crucial to the *continuity of the company*. It is exactly within this field of tension that processes for CR and stakeholder engagement seem to develop.

The instrumental documents for CR policies (business principles, often manifested in a code of conduct, operational guidelines and audit reports) seem to be closely interconnected with respect to the topics discussed and the related implementation processes. The process of developing these operational and instrumental documents seems to constitute a learning cycle within the companies. The effects of the CR policies formulated in operational guidelines are reviewed in audit reports that are used as input for the organisational learning process of assessing the overall CR policy and the operational guidelines. Two (out of seven) companies have gone through intensive internal and external processes of designing CR policies, and of explicit and audited reporting. They have reached levels of CR robustness internally and externally, allowing them to rely on internal stability in this area and to consciously have interactive stakeholder involvement.[4] Other companies are in advanced stages of this learning process. All reviewed companies claim to have gained organisational strength, quality and professionalism as a result of the ongoing internal processes towards CR policies. Also, all reviewed companies claim that there is no reason to fear an open and external communication process on CR policies, as long as a good internal process of change exists.

There is a need in companies for close collaboration with stakeholders to identify relevant issues, and to establish the relative importance of these issues. Also, it is necessary to actively promote the awareness and handling ability of CR-related issues within the organisation. The design of appropriate routines to match external demands with internal organisational capacities is equally necessary. As the company is informed about what the outside world thinks and what is expected from the organisation, stakeholders are made aware of the dilemmas companies face. Dialogue establishes a sense of understanding and can result in a change of attitude at both ends.

It is necessary to distinguish between issues of short-term relevance (usually company reputation), and those pertaining to the position of the company in the long run. On both counts, companies report the necessity to organise a bottom-up process within the organisation in order to determine relevant CR issues, as it is essential to accurately identify possible CR dilemmas. Research also showed that to employees, CR issues are real business issues that require the explicit acknowledgement of management. Management must set the stage but the determination of issues and the design of policies is an ongoing process at all levels of the organisation.

Short-term reputation issues are mostly directly recognisable as vivid business cases. The issues relevant for the long-term continuity of the company are often relatively obscure and require intensive processes for collaborative stakeholder engagement to become more lucid.

At the working level, employees are most often confronted with the reality of CR issues. Therefore, information on CR dilemmas in business units determines the importance of these issues for employees. Most companies report that internal processes often start with the analysis of questionnaires aimed at collecting information on CR issues. In addition, internal consultation processes and pilot studies to identify relevant CR business cases are deployed. In all investigated enterprises these internal processes worked to identify new issues.

Independent review of the results of the internal questionnaires and pilot investigations of CR issues by external consultants is an important condition to ensure transparency and employee collaboration. The process must be initiated and monitored by independent control and auditing services, including compulsory reporting to the top management. To address the issues that are identified via this process involves bringing the issues to the employees by means of, for instance, discussion groups or training programs. The election of change agents at the right level of management is crucial to start and empower an internal process based on continuous maintenance of the process and active support of the board. Training, monitoring and reporting are crucial elements of the CR process of organisational learning. Such internal processes enable the identification of relevant CR business cases and design of appropriate policies. Developing CR policies in the company is an educational process for both the business units and the corporate level. A *process* can be arranged to arrive at acceptable solutions, thus it is necessary to treat CR issues as business dilemmas. This requires the training of staff to recognise these issues and to handle such dilemmas. To support this work, a set of compact business principles and detailed guidelines on CR issues accompanied the internal change process of CR at all levels in the companies observed. Organisational learning processes take time, and investigation of these companies reported that allowing the organisation sufficient time to make the required adjustments is crucial.

Most companies investigated faced the problem of developing a *global* CR policy when local business units have a high degree of autonomy, often caused by *differences in perceptions.* Managers disagreed over what the facts were, how they were to be interpreted, and who was responsible for solving the problem. When all these disagreements were unearthed and discussed openly, the companies reviewed suggested that solutions become possible. Other learning points included that the central office cannot force a uniform CR package on all business units, as not all CR issues are equally important for all business units. In such instances, prioritising the findings of operational management is a suggested approach, allowing different priorities in different business units in line with the company's overall policy for CR. Again, *open discussion* can help determine the hurdles and identify how local adaptations to CR policies can be made and what partial successes can be achieved.

Value drivers for stakeholder approaches and CR policies

There are different clusters of value drivers for the development of CR strategies:

- Management of the company's external reputation in the *short term*;
- Management of the creation of improved conditions for business in the *long term*.

These two distinct clusters of arguments require intensive engagement in stakeholder approach and a divergent stakeholder approach.

The multinational companies participating in the research are most sensitive to incidents regarding CR issues. They carry A-brand products worldwide, and have business units run by partly independent management. Both aspects make the corporate reputation vulnerable. Elements close to the core business (e.g. health risks, food safety, environmental hazards) that might affect the customer's faith in the company were therefore key issues of concern. In addition, the companies reported that they were sensitive to stakeholder pressure to express opinions on new social or ethical and environmental issues in advance of adequate government regulations. The intensity of these pressures on company reliability is highlighted by the business adage of one of the companies, 'Business always comes back to you but credibility is lost forever.' CR issues are seldom restricted to the company alone. They increasingly require good mechanisms for discussion, monitoring and control of companies in the business chain as a whole, which was reported as a most relevant situation by all the companies in our research. And all companies involved in the research agreed that showing that organisational structures were in place to allow for adequate dilemma analysis in case of potential crises is key.

Those companies that have an advanced CR reputation tend to regard CR issues *and stakeholder management* for the protection of the company's *reputation* as business-as-usual proceedings. Companies in many instances expect to cover short-term reputation risks with regular business agendas. These routines pertain to the development of an adequate internal organisation of CR awareness, as well as to the need for continuous interactive work on good stakeholder relationships to understand stakeholder demands and to ensure a solid relational potential to manage surprise CR incidents. All companies involved in the research put in place organisational routines to deal with short-term reputation issues.

The companies in the study identified the creation of adequate conditions for economic continuity as the most important motivating value driver to engage in stakeholder approaches to CR strategy development. The majority of value drivers that were identified pertained to aspects of economic continuity, while a minority established issues of short-term concern. The companies found it difficult to develop thorough *stakeholder engagement* processes to identify changing demands and therefore it was equally difficult to identify the threats and opportunities for the company's continuity and long-term success. Seven companies in the study partly succeeded in integrating stakeholder views into a vision of their values and purposes. They considered this as a prerequisite to ensure their continuity, but experienced difficulties in opening up for new stakeholder groups. The companies involved were in different stages of a stakeholder approach that they all considered was an irreversible learning process towards increased levels of CR and sustainable entrepreneurship. CR policy development requires careful and thorough processes for organisational learning and network development (see also Clarke and Roome 1999; Boons and Berends 2001: 115).

Most companies expressed the importance of advanced CR practices for strengthening the socioeconomic conditions for business in general, both nationally and internationally. In addition, they expressed the importance of CR policies to contribute to the maintenance of ecological conditions to ensure business access to resources for long-term continuity. Companies find that a stakeholder approach in the development of CR strategies generates valuable information about the functioning of the organisation and the developments in the relevant CR issues of its direct and intermediate stakeholders. Important practical examples to engage in a stakeholder approach for reasons of continuity relate to community development programs, projects to improve employability and labour conditions nationally and internationally, programs to enhance health and safety conditions, projects for the preservation of ecological resources, and programs of product stewardship for sustainable technology development.

The seven multinationals in the study share a dominant strategic business focus on the continuity of the company that pressures them to continually analyse the long-term demands of their stakeholders as potential 'limitations' for future development. These companies range in durability, as mentioned in the analysis by Collins and Porras (1998). The empirical analysis emphasised the importance of long-term value drivers (in addition to short-term reputation management) to engage in collaborative stakeholder approach and CR policy development. Companies in the study all have a long term focus to work towards the optimisation of the values of *all* stakeholders they engage with, to ensure their own continuity as well as the continuity of meeting the interests of their stakeholders. The issues of short-term reputation management and long-term development of adequate conditions for continuity often conflict, but together constitute the prerequisites for proper functioning of the company. The dominance and importance of long-term value drivers for CR policy development compared to short-term drivers underlines the conclusion of Collins and Porras:

> Managers at visionary companies simply do not accept the proposition that they must choose between short-term performance or long-term success. They build first and foremost for the long term while simultaneously holding themselves to highly demanding short-term standards
>
> (Collins and Porras 1998: 192)

The companies investigated are beyond the stage of merely managing short-term interests of stakeholders, as short-term reputation management is reasonably under control. They are now engaging in lasting stakeholder relationships to understand the changing interests of stakeholders and, therefore, for good business-economic reasons, the changing interests of the company itself. The CR issues of national and international sustainable development contain important elements for renewal of business strategies to enhance continuity of business in the long term.

Recommendations on a stakeholder approach for CR business strategies

Empirical and theoretical research arrives at a number of recommendations on a stakeholder approach for the development of CR business policies. These recommendations relate to two business management issues:

1 the evaluation of value drivers for short-term and long-term business conditions;
2 the improvement of the business organisation to handle stakeholder demands.

Safeguarding the company's short-term CR reputation is a matter of regular business management aimed at avoiding economic damage to the business. Such routines must at least ensure the company's ability to avoid or adequately manage CR incidents close to the core business on, for instance, safety, health, labour conditions, environment and issues of company integrity. To this end, the company can proactively build and maintain stakeholder relationships with core interest groups to understand the evolving interests of a growing number of stakeholders. It also requires that companies stay visibly in tune with peer companies. Companies can work to implement organisational structures to determine and handle these CR issues in order to enable them to balance potentially conflicting stakeholder interests while guaranteeing that certain stakeholder demands can be met at certain acceptable minimal levels.

Handling long-term interests of stakeholders and the company requires lasting relationships between the two. Engaging in such deep and robust relationships with the aim of collaborating in the development of business strategies for continuity is an intensive and committed process. The issues of sustainability that increasingly dominate the CR business agenda all relate to very complicated long-term cross-sectoral interests that require equally complex organisational change processes. These processes must allow time for trust-building between company representatives and the related stakeholder groups to engage stakeholders and must be aimed at building mutual respect and developing shared values between the stakeholders and the company.

Senior management can enhance the change process by actively showing their commitment to CR issues, demonstrating respect for the values of the company's stakeholders, and by being explicit about the importance of collaborative stakeholder processes for the development of CR policies and for the business strategy in general.

The CR processes for a stakeholder approach need to be guided by internal staff and should aim at installing adequate business routines to safeguard short-term reputation issues, and achieve processes for interactive stakeholder engagement determining long-term business strategies.

For the successful design of an internal implementation process of CR policies six important elements are identified:

1   Start the process at the top and ensure the continuous support by the senior management for the change process of developing and implementing CR policies. Once the internal organisational change process has started, there is no way back.
2   The process needs to be guided by staff (by carefully selected 'change agents' in the business units). It is a continuous line-process of organisational learning and action-learning networks, and not a finite staff project. The process needs to be transparent, monitored, audited and reported upon.
3   Questionnaires and pilot studies in business units are necessary tools to define and focus the CR issues as true business issues for employees.
4   The process is time consuming; allow the time to set priorities, and identify involved business units, countries and regions. Parallel and diverging international trajectories can develop.
5   Diverging cultural and regional policies are needed (in particular in businesses in non-Western countries). Implementing policies in businesses that are not fully owned and have a different company culture require more attention and more time. New cultural attitudes can never be forced and always require acceptance.
6   Focus on structured organisational change, aiming to improve long-term economic conditions of the company. Focus on dilemmas, and show short-term and long-term potentials of CR policies.

External dialogue focuses on the explicit development of the collective learning cycles of evolving projects and programs, in which stakeholders and company representatives learn to jointly craft and implement new policies for progressive steps towards CR policies for sustainable development. Plotting of new business directions requires interactive shifting of company 'limitations' expressed in the expectations and demands of stakeholders. The complex business challenge is the ability to understand present and potential stakeholder demands, and the willingness to overcome such obstacles in creative and open change processes of joint learning. When companies aim for long-term success and continuity, they must improve the level of knowledge and ability in their organisation, enabling staff to understand the company's 'limitations' and to build strategies to shift these. Responding to and understanding stakeholder demands requires the highest degree of professionalism in the organisation on a great variety of issues in order to create the business conditions for continuity.

CR strategies require a full understanding of stakeholder interests and the company's ability to engage in dialogue and joint learning processes with the changing and widening array of stakeholders. Enterprises need to be open and willing to learn in interactive stakeholder approaches at the levels of the direct physical and social surroundings of the firm, of the supply and technology chains, and of the total production and consumption systems, including the private and public firms providing and developing infrastructural services. Firms can develop an approach to stakeholders with a focus on jointly developing and maintaining a collective learning cycle where progressive steps can be made toward CR policies for economic continuity and social and ecological value creation and a sustainable development. Connecting internal processes to this collective learning cycle is vital.

For the successful design of an external implementation process of CR policies there are four important elements:

1   Show, at all times, respect for the values and interests of customers, stakeholders and pressure groups. Know the evolving stakeholders' landscape and build on open and proactive relationships. Continuously review this landscape, check the relevance of present stakeholder groups and gauge the relevance of potential newcomers, especially with respect to issues pertaining to production conditions relevant for the long-term continuity of the company.

2   Customers and stakeholders expect firms to show their commitment to strengthen the social fabric of the community and to ensure the

availability of and access to ecological resources. Enterprises must show that they have a listening ear and a keen eye for such issues.

3 Take the initiative in external communications and prevent critical stakeholders from forcing the company into a defensive position. Remain able to set the agenda in a planned communication strategy. Always involve the representative bodies of employees in the internal process right from the start, and regularly involve external stakeholders consulting them and informing them on the developments.

4 External dialogues involve learning circles. Design the external process are a two-way and ongoing continuous communication and action-learning process. The dialogue can be used to share dilemmas in crafting and implementing the new policies.

Business principles and codes of conduct can be passively made public at fairly early stages, if their announcement can be combined with information on the ongoing internal change process of CR. Along the process the external dialogue can become more thorough and will leave room for agreement to disagree. Having an evolving process in place seems sufficient to be a respectable partner for stakeholder and pressure groups.

7   Summary of conclusions

Answering the research questions

The increasing complexity of sustainable development processes makes it necessary to intensify the collaboration between parties to ensure effective, committed and enduring change. This applies to the development of government policies and also to business strategies for sustainability. The research questions of this study were formulated as:

1   How does the complex and broadening range of sustainability issues affect policy processes for governments and businesses?
2   How can enterprises manage the strategic processes of adapting their resources and capabilities to the new sustainability demands from a growing number of stakeholders?

The issues related to sustainable development are expanding to include issues of local and global environmental qualities, the preservation of energy resources, minerals and biodiversity, and the management of socioeconomic development. The related involvement of government and business policy processes requiring input from a growing number of stakeholders has also grown more complex. The present sustainability problems relate to cross-sectoral issues, simultaneously affecting economic, social and ecological interests, and require fact finding, risk analysis operations and joint resolution processes.

A collaborative stakeholder and consensus building approach on the part of governments and businesses is a necessary condition to create *commitment* to a solid foundation of policies and strategies for sustainability. In addition, such a collaborative stakeholder approach supports governments and businesses in creating the necessary *joint learning* processes for the development of sustainable strategies and policies. Elements like *commitment* and *joint learning* in collaborative stakeholder approaches are essential for the development of effective and enduring sustainability policies.

Companies must now learn to understand and incorporate the demands of their stakeholders. And companies need to build strategies to ensure their sustainability. Also, government and business are facing the challenge of sustainable development signalled by a new agenda for ecological and social modernisation. The key words of this wave of government policies and business strategies for sustainable development include:

- extension and intensification of a *collaborative stakeholder approach* to engage new stakeholders in the development of innovative government policies and business strategies for sustainability; and
- *transition* to sustainable technologies for production and new technology systems.

Considered together, the central conclusions of this study (and answers to the two research questions posed at the beginning of this chapter) indicate that:

1 Issues of sustainable development have grown too complex to be resolved by single parties in society and require close collaboration between all societal parties.
2 Sustainable companies develop strategies to enhance the flexibility of their resources and engage stakeholders in joint commitment and joint learning processes.

The first conclusion: the complexity of issues of sustainable development

The historical development of environmental policies provides a number of learning points related to the advantages of involving a diversity of interests in the consensus-building processes for the development of environmental policies. Until the end of the 1980s the key lesson learned from environmental policy development established that stakeholders (people, businesses and governments) must be encouraged and enabled to integrate environmental concerns into their regular decision-making efforts. Engaging stakeholders in risk assessment, for instance, was found to greatly enhance their commitment to implementing the resulting policies. Communicating the benefits of maintaining environmental qualities and environmental resources to stakeholders was also a key lesson.

In the last decade of environmental policy development, it is clear that cross-sectoral interests need to represent ecological, economic and social challenges simultaneously. Within the ecological arena, encouraging autonomy at the local government level is a necessary step to effectively resolve interconnected socioeconomic and environmental issues. The Netherlands government successfully encourages such mandates to local governments for setting environmental targets and limits, and balancing local environmental concerns with related social, health and economic interests. Also offered by the Dutch government, the covenant process grants greater autonomy to industry for designing environmental business policies.

The comprehensive focus of the environmental policy development agenda of governments and businesses in the past decades continues to expand. While the *Brundtland Report* calls for a combination of seemingly inconsistent objectives, present political debates on sustainable development assume some form of intergenerational responsibility and connection. Political debates on sustainable development have become more explicitly focused on intergenerational responsibilities and the implied uncertainties of the impact on future production possibilities based on present technologies and consumption patterns.

The ethics of managing public goods, including natural, economic, social and institutional capital, is characterised by a sense of responsibility for ensuring the good of present and future generations. These ethics are participatory in nature, requiring a collective responsibility for and close co-operation between all societal parties. Susskind's analysis is most applicable to the current complex business conditions, proposing such participatory approaches for situations in which the solution to a problem is not immediately clear to all affected parties or in which people disagree on the best solution or decision. This is emphasised by the fact that present conventional institutions are not able to handle the complex long-term ecological and socioeconomic dilemmas represented by intergenerational responsibility.

The concept of 'participatory ethics' calls for processes where enterprises, governments and non-governmental organisations (NGOs) share responsibilities. The purpose is to generate solutions for dilemmas that are challenging to all parties, and to engage all partners in achieving shared objectives. Underlining the importance of new forms and fora to arrange for intense, open and democratic debate on ecological risk analysis and ecological and economic modernisation is also important to consider. The proposals, as expressed by Von Schomberg, for a 'deliberative societal opinion development' to debate and to handle uncertainties and risks in ecological and technological decision-making processes in a new 'third arena' of societal conflict management are also central.

At present, government processes (in the Netherlands) are evolving to design policy that engages the widest array of stakeholders. The aim is to enable the effective handling of long-term sustainability issues such as climate change, loss of biodiversity, exploitation of natural (mineral) resources, and potentially uncontrollable risks of the use of hazardous chemicals. As an example, the recent Dutch National Environmental Policy Plan (NEPP4) analyses the potential ecological dilemmas for the next three decades and formulates a provisional 'quality perspective' for the year 2030. It shows the need for long-term processes for designing innovative technological systems, and at the same time realises conditions for economic feasibility and social and cultural acceptability. The plan also proposes to implement processes of transition towards sustainable energy use, sustainable use of mineral resources, sustainable agriculture and sustainable natural resource management and infrastructure development. Drawing heavily on active participation of the private sector in developing the process of ecological modernisation and of shaping intergenerational responsibility, it is an example of 'participatory ethics'.

The 'transition processes' for the development and introduction of sustainable technological systems requires the inclusion of many stakeholders and time for risk assessment of potential threats and policy solutions. In analysing the transition process towards sustainable business, companies need to collaborate in joint societal policy development processes, and engage in strategic alliances for the accelerated development of sustainable infrastructures for energy, transport, communication, education and technology. In the final analysis, these elements determine the possibilities for sustainable production.

The rapid changes in industrialised countries with respect to sustainable technology transitions and production practices, and the increasing need for companies to expand into new markets in developing countries, presents a range of new management issues and an increasing number of stakeholders. The new demands companies are faced with urge them to renew their business strategies in order to ensure continuity of business in the long run. The minimum requirement for continuity in industrialised markets is a broadening of stakeholder relationships in order to consider such issues as technology and infrastructure development for the sustainable production of energy, transport, chemicals and food, and for nature conservation. In addition, diverse stakeholder relationships are necessary to understand and utilise the market growth potential in countries in transition and in the Third World. Transition management at company level requires a vision with long-term objectives, and identifying potential short-term gains from change processes towards a sustainable enterprise.

The second conclusion: strategies to enhance flexibility of the sustainable enterprise

In addition to the investigation of macro sustainability perspectives for governments and businesses, looking at micro perspectives is essential. Micro business perspectives can support the realisation of sustainable business practices.

Sustainable development demands extensive change and innovation of products and markets. Companies that are able to understand the sustainability signals from changing sets of stakeholder groups, and are equipped to adjust their resources to meet the new demands, can be at an advantage in transitioning to sustainable business actions. Strategic sustainable management requires the highest performance in terms of product innovation, production processes, market reorientation and stakeholder engagement. And this requires an integration of business management strategies.

Further, it is observed that business strategies for sustainability do not differ greatly from general business strategies. The key difference is the reaction to changing market and regulatory demands that enhance sustainable conditions for ecological preservation and social equity. As mentioned before, these issues of sustainability create a degree of pressure on the company's strategic management and require continuous assessment of a company's capability to direct and adjust its distinctive resources to the changing demands of sustainability in the markets it is operating in or considers operating in. According to resource-based views, analysis of a company's strategic strengths and weaknesses requires assessment of the value and adaptability of its resources and capabilities in all the parts of the value chain, with respect to its ability to respond to external threats and opportunities. The strategic audit is an important element in building business strategies. Such audits address questions such as:

• What are the company's distinctive capabilities?
• Are the markets that the company operates in benefiting from its distinctive capability to add value?
• Are there any other markets in which the company is not yet active where it might enjoy competitive advantage (the question of identification of new opportunities in present or new markets)?

- How can competitive advantage be sustained and appropriated (the question of analysis of potential threats of new entries, potential substitutes, suppliers and customers)?

This analysis can lead to a number of recommendations to improve the internal strategy development of enterprises. The company's internal organisation structures can be equipped to systematically investigate the ecological and business horizon of the firm to identify relevant discontinuities and opportunities in both areas. It is also essential that companies systematically chart their regular business and stakeholder relations to identify potential new players in supply and technology chains. Companies can consider these change processes as continuous learning cycles within action learning networks of companies and stakeholders.

Subsequently, the stakeholder approach for the development of sustainable business strategies is more than a simple response to stakeholder demands, and requires a long-term strategy to plot the interests of the company as well as stakeholder demands in the long run. Long-term stakeholder interests share the direction of change toward sustainability that can be established while the objectives for sustainability in general, and for long-term success of the firm, remain elusive. The exact meaning and importance of these objectives needs to develop in societal processes balancing ecological, social and economic demands, accounting for future economic and technological opportunities.

The *transition* to sustainable business requires the *plotting* of a new direction by engaging the stakeholders of the company to understand needs and to develop common goals. It is equally important to achieve appropriate social, ecological and economic conditions and technical infrastructures for future production. Therefore, the central concern of the company is to understand its stakeholders, and to continue satisfying stakeholder objectives, thus creating the right conditions for sustainability.

From the theoretical and empirical perspectives, a collaborative stakeholder approach is vital for developing business strategies for sustainability, as well as for creating the right business conditions for long-term continuity. Business strategies for sustainable development aim to achieve the essential conditions for long-term continuity of the company, and a stakeholder approach is crucial to determine the related requirements. The complex business challenge here is nothing less than the ability to understand present and potential stakeholder demands, and the willingness to address issues in a creative and open change processes. When companies aim for long-term success and continuity they also need to strive to improve the level of knowledge and ability in their organisation, enabling staff to understand the company's 'limitations' and to build strategies to shift these.

Suggestions for further research

The movement towards sustainable development continues to evolve. National legislation and international conventions on sustainable development, and market demand for sustainable products and sustainable production processes, drive today's business agendas. Governments are working to arrange and manage the related public change processes and guide the required societal processes for the development of new technologies and infrastructures, enabling sustainable production processes and consumption patterns. At the same time, the private sector is confronted with an equally complicated agenda to participate in the societal transition processes and to achieve the development toward sustainable business.

From these learning points, a number of considerations on the development of collaborative stakeholder approaches and consensus building processes emerge. These questions relate to three distinct areas of research: public management of change processes, business management of strategic change, and questions on business ethics.

Analysis suggests that the required transition processes toward sustainable infrastructures for the production of energy, transportation and food, and the preservation of resources, biodiversity and space, necessarily involve a multitude of cross-sectoral social, ecological and economic interests. These interrelated interests imply the presence of large numbers of stakeholders and therefore contain potential conflicts of interests.

Investigating appropriate methods for governments to develop and manage such complex societal processes is essential. This is necessary to gain better insight for governments to identify the right partners for these transition processes, and to establish the potential interest in commitment to action. The related technological and sociocultural changes require extensive investment from governments, business and people in the short term. At the same time, the economic risks are substantial as there is no guarantee that these investments produce results in the long run. Procedures enabling the identification of the right partners and measures of the effectiveness of these change processes require intensive further research.

New procedures are desirable to enable the identification and inclusion of interest groups to assess potential risks and responses to these issues. As such, consensus building theories as methodological processes deserve further analysis in the support of complex multi-stakeholder processes of shared information collection, bridging 'knowledge gaps' and joint risk assessments.

Governments may benefit from further research in the design of action-learning networks for the development of sustainable technology systems and infrastructures. A great deal remains to be learned about the potential of new action partnerships among industry, research and finance, which should go beyond the present traditional networks. Important questions in this area relate to overcoming competitive boundaries between companies and developing partnerships across industries and sectors. The same applies to questions to overcome national attitudes that may impede the development of desirable cross-border facilities for sustainable development.

Equally important is research into enhancing risk-assessment and cost–benefit considerations for adopting degrees of sustainable behaviour within limits of evolving macro targets of sustainable development by people and companies. Further investigation into the potentials of the allocation of property rights, in, for instance, systems of tradable emissions and use rights, is also of value as these new instruments may prove indispensable in guiding the democratic processes of sharing the benefits and risks of sustainable development paths. Governments also need new legal and economic instruments to allow for the great diversity in risk perceptions and risk preparedness. Instruments that allow for this greater diversity in individual behaviour may enhance processes of change.

Changing demands from governments and markets for sustainable products and production processes, and changing business opportunities arising from new sustainable technological production possibilities, confront businesses with strategic management decisions. The demands of sustainable development place pressure on organisations, as they require fundamental changes in production technology, involve considerable risks and uncertainties, and require application of complex production procedures to allow for the influence of a growing number of external stakeholders.

Related to these demands, it is essential to develop an understanding of

- the internal organisation of new processes and procedures to allow for sustainable business practices;
- the management of external engagement in stakeholder networks in order to learn about their changing demands and expectations;

- the management of dialogues, the interface, between the firm's internal organisation and its external stakeholders.

Research into organisational learning processes remains crucial for the development of the complex organisational changes toward the sustainable enterprise. Further research is required on how 'general' management strategies can be applied in order to increase the company's flexibility in rearranging its resources and capabilities for sustainability, and to enable innovative processes for product and market development. Such research relates to experiences of management processes for innovation within the company, and also pertains to collaborative management processes within the broader networks of value and technology chains. Research into alternative management systems for product and market development under different economic conditions in enterprises, with respect to varying degrees of competition intensity, or varying degrees of collaboration between enterprises, is also promising.

The adequate engagement of stakeholders is vital for change and innovation processes within the sustainable enterprise. The design of adequate collaborative stakeholder processes for the development and introduction of sustainable technology systems and infrastructures (allowing for future sustainable production processes), in particular, leaves many open research questions. This applies to processes at the individual company level, to groups of enterprises linked in shared supply and technology chains, and to production sectors linked in competing networks. Identifying the conditions for enterprises to engage in action learning networks requires further research.

Also, investigating the potential of cross-sectoral interests and related collaborative company processes in differing sectors, such as sustainable technologies and infrastructures, may provide a cross-sectoral perspective. Research into potential interests of different industries and supporting financial services of banks and governments might render interesting results for promoting organisational support for sustainable businesses.

Finally, understanding how organisational structures enhance the connection between action learning networks for the sustainable business and internal organisational learning and adjustment processes of the company is a focus of value.

The basic issues of sustainable development pertain to questions regarding the preservation of production and carrying capacity for future generations. These questions present complicated considerations on the responsibility of private enterprises in an open and free market economy that deserve further investigation.

This signals the need for further research into the business implications of the precautionary principle, including questions about the development of adequate institutional arrangements to allow for the participation of businesses in debates and resolution processes on issues of sustainability. Today, companies are responsible for their business actions and how they influence others (like suppliers or customers).

Issues of sustainable development and corporate social responsibility are related to economic and social systems, and also increasingly in the confrontation of economic and cultural systems. These interactions also reflect unique emotions, desires and values of relationships and movements of people. These characteristics influence the behaviour of companies as responsible world citizens. Also related are the present normative stakeholder dialogues between companies and 'established' NGOs. These new dialogues may develop a focus less on 'norms' and more on 'values', worldviews and meaning. Thus, business ethics can make important contributions to the societal debate by identifying dilemmas and underlying assumptions, and extending the range of ethical principles in business to include the rights and interests of future generations.

Notes

1 Introduction

1   There are three different reference names for the publications of the Ministry of the Environment: VROM, Ministry of the Environment, and Ministry of Housing, Spatial Planning and Environmental Protection. All three names are correct, and throughout the text the use of 'VROM' is used as the reference in the reference section to refer to the Dutch Ministry of Housing, Spatial Planning and Environmental Protection.

2 The changing ecological arena

1   After 1972, when the Environmental Protection Department was established as a separate body within the Ministry of Public Health Care, the following major legislation passed: Seawater Pollution Act (1975), Wastes Act (1975), Environmentally Hazardous Substances Act (1976), Noise Nuisance Act (1979), Groundwater Act (1981) and Soil Cleanup Act (1982).
2   The radical transition in the Netherlands during the 1970s from coal to natural gas (which was discovered in the Netherlands in the 1960s) may have been as influential as legislation in reducing emissions of heavy metals and SO_2. Also, the oil crises of the mid-1970s enhanced energy-saving measures. Indeed, the resulting increased energy prices and the shock of the oil boycott by the Arab countries in 1973 challenged the Dutch people's belief that they had guaranteed access to endlessly available fossil fuels and other resource stocks.
3   Data from the International Committee for the Protection of the Rhine River in Koblenz, Germany, report that oxygen levels in the Rhine went up from an all-time low of 4.8 milligrams per liter (mpl) in 1971 to 8 mpl in 1980 and 9.8 mpl in 1995. This steady and significant improvement led to the return of salmon and sea trout in this river.
4   On the basis of their comprehensive database, policy makers in the Environmental Protection Department (VROM) were able to clearly define and locate the required cleanup operations and identify the sources of pollution. It became possible to precisely indicate the size, location and origin of the problems at the level of groups of enterprises and consumers.

Thus the art of making environmental policy became highly profession-alised. Most of the problems put on the table in negotiation processes regarding the origin of and responsibility for pollution could be defined and addressed. At the same time (and just as important), the Netherlands' National Research Institute for Public Health and the Environment (RIVM) and VROM developed an impressive database of potential measures that could be implemented, including assessments of their environmental effect and the costs involved.

5   It would take, however, until 1992 before the Netherlands' Parliament formally approved of this road to engage stakeholders through voluntary agreements. They previously asserted that all agreements were to be sent to Parliament for scrutiny. Environmental groups initially regarded volun-tary agreements with great unease, claiming that government was giving away its regulatory powers.

6   NEPP3 said in 1998: 'The philosophy on the role of legislation as a management instrument is changing. The long gestation period of legislation and its lack of flexibility mean that legislation is more often seen as constraining social innovation ... There is a need for innovative regulatory instruments for the 21st century which will promote and facilitate greater autonomy on the part of the regional and local authorities and target groups, and will be more oriented towards safeguarding the quality of the living environment' (VROM 1998a: 216).

7   NEPP1 started this process of developing covenants on an experimental basis as part of the regulatory licensing system. It would develop to become the core of environmental management, formally acclaimed in the sub-sequent NEPPs and the Environmental Management Act.

8   These negotiated agreements, which were at the core of the implemen-tation process, allowed for greater flexibility in the timing and framing of changes in production processes. The agreements enabled corporate officials to use their best judgment in making these changes, rather than having government prescribe them. In this way, private enterprises could apply new technologies and change production processes according to their business planning, not top-down regulation. At the same time, government officials were assured that the knowledge and capabilities of private enterprise would be utilised to the greatest possible extent, and that process times were much shorter than if legislation were developed. In addition (and perhaps most important), private enterprise developed clear responsibilities for the environment through this approach; they showed true commitment. The threat of weak compromises could be handled, and strong monitoring and evaluation programs made it possible to firmly guide and check the progress of these negotiated agreements. It is difficult to tell whether these agreements sufficiently supported the introduction of regime-shift technologies or merely strengthened the diffusion of available technologies.

9   Evaluation of the progress of environmental management after the NEPP1 had shown that: 'Three hard conditions must be met for environmental policy to prompt target groups to take measures: clear targets (what has to be achieved), adequate technologies and facilities (how can we achieve it), and adequate degree of certainty over the usefulness and permanence of the measures (why is it necessary).' For point sources, these conditions

were met, but for diffuse sources (SMEs and consumers) this could not be achieved by means of covenants or regulation. Indirect fiscal, economic and social instruments needed to be developed to reach these target groups. Also, the development of proper facilities to allow for adjustment of environmental behaviour needed to be improved (VROM 1993a: 34).

10 The 'Towns and Environment Project' was set up as an experiment in NEPP2 in 1993 (VROM 1993a: 199). The experiment was conducted in 25 selected areas from 1995 to 1998. NEPP3 in 1998 reports on the follow-up program (VROM 1998a: 197). Two other key projects gave local authorities greater latitude in policy-making processes: the 'BEVER project' to differentiate soil standards according to the function of the land (VROM 1998a: 167–72) and the 'MIG project' to use differential noise pollution standards (VROM 1998a: 180–2).

11 This estimate was obtained by counting the technology-based instruments and measures included in the list of 223 actions in NEPP1.

12 Lawrence Susskind in 'Super-optimization: a new approach to national environmental policy-making' (a paper delivered to the 'Seminar on Sustainable Development: Towards a New Balance Between Environment, Economy and Social Welfare', sponsored by the Ministry of Housing, Physical Planning and Environmental Protection, The Hague, The Netherlands, January 1999) claims as follows: 'Many policy analysts believe strongly that the gains in environmental protection achieved over the last decade or two have come at the expense of economic growth and improved social welfare. Political conservatives often do not accept the argument that the achievement of environmental protection might bring with it new opportunities for economic development as well as improvements in social welfare. It is now time ... to ensure that all future efforts to enhance environmental quality guarantee economic improvement and enhance social welfare. One way to move in this direction is to adopt an approach to policy-making called super-optimization' (Susskind 1999: 1)

13 NEPP3 includes a long list of potential measures to be taken to meet the Kyoto objectives (VROM 1998a: 138) and shows how it impinges on economic and social interests. These measures include a reduction of maximum speeds, increased excises on gasoline (causing gas prices to rise from US$4 to $5 per gallon), very costly substitution of gas for coal in electricity production, and new and expensive technologies for underground storage of CO_2.

14 Recent studies indicate that under certain conditions, even now, air transportation has a more favourable energy profile than rail transportation. These profiles are rapidly changing due to new air and rail technologies. Centrum voor Energiebesparing en Schone Energie (Centre for Energy Saving and Clean Energy), Delft, The Netherlands is at present engaged in research into these phenomena.

3 Future generations and business ethics

1 This chapter was co-authored with Professor Dr R. Jeurissen of Nyenrode University.

2 The final political declaration of the World Summit on Sustainable Development (the 'Johannesburg Declaration') names as one of the five

core challenges the protection of the planet's natural resources. The declaration says: 'Loss of biodiversity continues, fish stocks continue to be depleted, desertification claims more and more fertile land, the adverse effects of climate change are already evident, natural disasters are more frequent and more devastating ...' (WSSD 2002). Since the publication of the Report of the Club of Rome (Meadows 1972) there has been a growing international concern over the intergenerational side to the preservation of resources. At first, the focus was mainly on the need to respond to the problems of environmental deterioration. Later, and especially after the publication of the *Brundtland Report* in 1987 (WCED 1987) and in the wake of the United Nations (UN) Conference on Environment and Development held in Rio de Janeiro in 1992, the international ecological concern broadened to include the preservation of resources, stocks of minerals, energy, water and biodiversity. Despite the scientific uncertainty of actual risks related to the potential losses of such resources, and despite the widely varying risk perceptions and risk attitudes of nations, these issues of preservation have steadily grown to become the central focus of international and national environmental policy. The 'precautionary principle' introduced as a guiding principle for the design of environmental policy in the Rio de Janeiro Summit in 1992 has since then become an important tool for handling policy issues of ecological uncertainty.

3   A future generation is 'some generation no members of which have presently been conceived and so in no sense presently exist' (De George 1979: 96). There is a stable consensus among theorists over the definition of 'future generation'. Golding defines future generations as 'generations with which the possessors of the obligations cannot expect in a literal sense to share a common life' (Golding 1981: 61–72). The most extensive definition is by De Shalit: 'A generation is a set of people who are more or less the same age and who live at the same period in history, usually regarded as having a span of thirty years. Future generations are people who by definition will live after contemporary people are dead' (De Shalit 1995: 138, note 1).

4   One of the few exceptions is Velasquez (1998: 290–4). However, Velasquez limits the responsibility to future generations to what is known as the 'campingside principle': we are to hand over to our immediate successors a world that is in no worse condition than the one we received from our ancestors (Velasquez 1998: 292). This view fails to take long-term, transgenerational environmental impacts into account. In an automated content analysis of two leading journals in the field of business ethics, *Business Ethics Quarterly* and *Journal of Business Ethics,* from their first issue onward, we found zero articles devoted to future generations. The content analysis was done with the help of the Proquest database.

5   During the past decades an extensive, but rather fragile, international legislative body has been built for the protection of biodiversity, despite the great number of uncertainties which surround these issues. The precautionary principle forms the policy foundation to prevent unnecessary damage to biodiversity, even though there is a great lack of clarity on the acceptable or minimum resource levels to sustain life-support functions of resources of biodiversity. This framework ensures that all nations take

appropriate steps to protect resources of biodiversity whenever they become endangered by actions or projects of people, businesses or governments, thus establishing an international connection to safeguard biodiversity as an interlinked global system.

4 The transition to the sustainable enterprise

1 The Factor 10 Club (Chair: F. Schmidt-Bleek) issued what is known as the 'Carnoules Declaration' in Wuppertal, Germany, in 1994.
2 The following paradigm shifts are dominant and recurrent trends identified in, e.g., the works of Elkington J. (1997) *Cannibals with forks*, Oxford: Capstone; Hawken P., Lovins, A.B. and Lovins, L. Hunter (1999) *Natural Capitalism, The Next Industrial Revolution*, London: Earthscan; Von Weiszacker E.U., Lovins, A.B. and Lovins, L.H. (1997) *Factor Four, Doubling Wealth – Halving Resource Use*, Munich: Earthscan.

5 Management strategies for sustainable businesses

1 This chapter was co-authored with Dr F. Boons, Senior Researcher at Erasmus University of Rotterdam
2 Analysis included the financial and environmental audit reports and other public information disseminated by these companies, as well as interviews with relevant company officials on the development of strategies for sustainability to determine the design and the advancement of business strategies towards sustainability. Conclusions were evaluated in workshops attended by the involved companies.

6 Plotting sustainable directions

1 The full research report is confidential. These companies were included because of their advanced reputation in the field of CR. The investigation included relevant public documents and websites of these companies, as well as interviews with managers responsible for CR policies.
2 Shell is active in the energy producing and distribution sector, ING is a bank and insurance company, Ahold is a major retailer, and the other enterprises are all actively engaged in the production of food and beverages.
3 Analysis included how CR policies, with respect to a number of issues related to the interests of internal and external stakeholders, are developed. Internally, the interests of shareholders on issues such as corporate governance and investor relations (e.g. regarding the position of shareholders and commissioners, the reporting and integrity of the financial records), and on the position and rights of employees (e.g. regarding policies of employment, employee representation, freedom of association, right to collective bargaining, handling of integrity issues on conflicts of interests, gifts and sexual harassment) were identified. Externally, the stakeholder interests of business partners, competitors, clients and society at large with respect to competitive attitudes (e.g. on fair competition, bribery and corruption, presence in politically sensitive regions, support of political

parties), quality and safety of products, ecological quality of production, and human rights (e.g. policies on non-discrimination and child-labour) were identified.

4   For an additional and specific analysis of the progress made at Shell also see Lawrence (2002).

References

Achterberg, W. (1994) *Samenleving, natuur en duurzaamheid: Een inleiding in de milieufilosofie* (in Dutch) [Society, nature and sustainability: An introduction to environmental philosophy], Assen: Van Gorcum.

Ansoff, H.I. (1965) *Corporate Strategy*, New York: McGraw Hill.

Ashford, N.A. (1994) 'An innovation-based strategy for the environment', in A.M. Finkel and D. Golding (eds) *Worst Things First*, Washington, DC: Resources for the Future.

Ayres, R.U. (1998) *Technology, Energy and Materials*, Rotterdam: OCFEB.

Ayres R.U., van den Bergh, J.C.J.M and Gowdy, J.M. (2001) 'Strong versus weak sustainability: economics, natural sciences, and "consilience"', *Environmental Ethics*, 23(Summer): 155–68.

Barney, J.B. (2002) *Gaining and Sustaining Competitive Advantage*, Upper Saddle River, NJ: Prentice Hall.

Barney J.B. and Arikan A.M. (2001) 'The resource based views: origin and implications', in M.A. Hitt, R.E. Freeman and J.S. Harrison (eds) *The Blackwell Handbook of Strategic Management*, Oxford: Blackwell Publishers.

Blackstone, W. (1974) 'Ethics and ecology', in W. Blackstone (ed.) *Philosophy and Environmental Crisis*, Athens, GA: University of Georgia Press.

Boons, F. and Berends, M. (2001) 'Stretching the boundary: the possibilities of flexibility as an organizational capability in industrial ecology', *Business Strategy and the Environment*, 10: 115–24.

Boons, F., Baas, L., Bouma, J.J., De Groene, A. and Le Blansch, K. (2001) *The Changing Nature of Business*, Utrecht: International Books.

Braungart, M. (1999) Speech delivered to the Seminar on Sustainable Development: Towards a New Balance between Environment, Economy, and Social Welfare, The Netherlands: VROM.

Braungart, M. and McDonough, W. (2000) 'A world of abundance', *Interfaces* (Special issue: Sustainable business), 30(3): 55–65.

Carpenter, S.R. (1998) 'Sustainability', in R. Chadwick (ed.) *The Encyclopedia of Applied Ethics*, San Diego: Academic Press.

Carrol, A.B. and Bucholtz, A.K. (2002) *Business and Society: Ethics and Stakeholder Management*, 5th edition, South Western: Mason.

Checkland, P. (1981) *Systems Thinking, Systems Practice*, Chichester: John Wiley and Sons.

Chisholm, R. (1998) *Developing Network Organizations*, Reading, MA: Addison Wesley.

Clarke, S. and Roome, N. (1999) 'Sustainable business: learning-action networks as organizational assets', *Business Strategy and the Environment*, 8(5): 296–310.

Collins, J.C. and Porras, J.I. (1996) *Built to Last*, London: Century.

Daly, H. (1997) 'Georgescu-Roegen versus Solow/Stiglitz, and Solow's reply', *Ecological Economics*, 22: 261–6.

Davidson, M.D (2000) 'Recht en duurzame ontwikkeling' (in Dutch) [Law and sustainable development], *Milieu en recht*, 4: 95–9.

De George, R. (1979) 'The environment, rights and future generations', in K. Goodpaster and K. Sayre (eds) *Ethics and Problems of the 21st Century*, Notre Dame: University of Notre Dame Press.

De Jongh, P. (1999) *Our Common Journey: A Pioneering Approach to Cooperative Management*, London: Zed Books.

De Koning, M. (1994) *In dienst van het milieu: Enkele memoires van oud directeur-generaal Prof. ir. W.C. Reij* (in Dutch) [In the service of the environment: Some memoires of former director-general Prof. ir. W.C. Reij], Alphen aan de Rijn: Samson, H.D. Tjeenk Willink.

De Shalit, A. (1995) *Why Posterity Matters: Environmental Policies and Future Generations*, London: Routledge.

Donaldson, T. (1989) *The Ethics of International Business*, New York: Oxford University Press.

Dutch Ministry of Economic Affairs (1996) *Third White Paper on Energy Policy*, available online at http://www.minez.nl.

Ekins, P. (2000) *Economic Growth and Environmental Sustainability*, London: Routledge.

Elkington, J. (1997) *Cannibals with Forks*, Oxford: Capstone.

EU (2001) *Sustainable Production: Challenges and Objectives for EU Research Policy*, Report of the expert group on competitive and sustainable production and related service industries in Europe in the period to 2020, Brussels: European Commission.

Feinberg, J. (1981) 'The rights of animals and unborn generations', in E. Partridge (ed.) *Responsibilities to Future Generations*, Buffalo: Prometheus Books.

Foster, J.M. (ed.) (1997) *Valuing Nature: Ethics, Economics and the Environment*, London: Routledge.

Freeman, R.E. (1984) *Strategic Management: A Stakeholder Approach*, Boston: Pitman.

Freeman, R.E. and McVea, J. (1984) *A Stakeholder Approach to Strategic Management*, Oxford: Blackwell Publishers.

Freeman, R.E. and McVea, J. (2001) A stakeholder approach to strategic management, in M.A. Hitt, R.E. Freeman and J.S. Harrison (eds) *The*

Blackwell Handbook of Strategic Management, Oxford: Blackwell Publishers.

Freeman, R.E., Pierce, J. and Dodd, R. (2000) *Environmentalism and the New Logic of Business*, Oxford: Oxford University Press.

Gladwin, T. (1995) 'Beyond eco-efficiency: towards socially sustainable business', *Sustainable Development*, 3(April): 35–43.

Gladwin, T., Krause, T.S. and Kennely, J. (1995) 'Shifting paradigms for sustainable development', *Academy of Management Review*, 20(4): 874–907.

Golding M.P. (1981) 'Obligations to future generations', in E. Partridge (ed.) *Responsibilities to Future Generations*, Buffalo: Prometheus Books.

Goodin, R.E. (1985) *Protecting the Vulnerable: A Reanalysis of our Social Responsibilities*, Chicago: University of Chicago Press.

Groen, M. (1988) *Naar een duurzaam Nederland* (in Dutch) [Towards a sustainable Netherlands], The Hague: SDU.

Harrison, J.S. and Freeman, R.E. (1999) 'Stakeholders, social responsibility, and performance: empirical evidence and theoretical perspectives', *Academy of Management Journal*, 42(5): 479–85.

Harrison, J.S. and St John, C.H. (1998) *Strategic Management of Organizations and Stakeholders*, Cincinnati: South-Western Publishing.

Hart, S.L. (1995) 'A natural-resource-based view of the firm', *Academy of Management Review*, 20(4): 986–1,014.

Hart, S.L. (1997) 'Beyond greening: strategies for a sustainable world', *Harvard Business Review*, Jan–Feb: 66–76.

Hart, S.L. and Milstein, M.B. (1999) 'Global sustainability and the creative destruction of industries', *Sloan Management Review*, Fall: 23–33.

Hawken, P. (2000) *Natural Capitalism: The Next Industrial Revolution*, London: Earthscan.

Howarth, R.B. (1992) 'Intergenerational justice and the chain of obligations', *Environmental Values*, 1: 133–40.

Jeurissen, R.J.M. (2002) *The Corporation as a Global Citizen* (Inaugural lecture), Nyenrode: Nyenrode University Press.

Jongh, de P. (1999) *Our Common Journey: A Pioneering Approach to Cooperative Environmental Management*, London: ZED Books.

Kay, J. (1996) *The Economics of Business*, Oxford: Oxford University Press.

Keijzers, G. (2000) 'The changing ecological arena from 1970–2000 and beyond', *Journal of Cleaner Production*, 8: 179–200

Keijzers, G. (2002) 'The transition to the sustainable enterprise', *Journal of Cleaner Production*, 10: 349–59.

Keijzers, G. (2003) 'Creating sustainable directions: evolving stakeholder approaches in seven multinationals', *The Journal of Corporate Citizenship*, 10(Summer): 79–88.

Keijzers, G., Boons, F. and Van Daal, R. (2002) *Duurzaam ondernemen: Strategie van bedrijven* (in Dutch) [Sustainable entrepreneurship: Strategies of corporations], Deventer: Kluwer.

Keijzers, G. and Jeurissen, R. (2002) *Duurzaam ondernemen: Toekomstethiek in dialoog* (in Dutch) [Sustainable entrepreneurship: future ethics in dialogue], Deventer: Kluwer.

Keijzers, G. and Jeurissen, R. (2004) 'Future generations and business ethics', *Business Ethics Quarterly*, 14 (1): 47–69.

Kennedy, P. (1993) *Preparing for the Twenty-first Century*, New York: Random House.

Kolk, A. (2000) *Economics of Environmental Management*, London: Pearson.

Kolk A. and Mauser A. (2002) 'The evolution of environmental management: from stage models to performance evaluation', *Business Strategy and the Environment*, 11: 4–31

Lawrence A.T. (2002) 'The drivers of stakeholder engagement', *Journal of Corporate Citizenship*, 6(Summer): 71–85.

Lee, K. (1998) 'Biodiversity', in R. Chadwick (ed.) *Encyclopedia of Applied Ethics*, Vol. I, San Diego: Academic Press.

Lomborg, B. (2001) *The Skeptical Environmentalist: Measuring the Real State of the World*, New York: Cambridge University Press.

Lovejoy, T. (2002) 'Biodiversity: dismissing scientific process', *Scientific American*, 286(1): 69–71.

Luper-Foy, S. (1995) 'International justice and the environment', in D.E. Cooper and J.A. Palmer (eds) *Just Environments*, London: Routledge.

Mac Lean, D. (1983) 'A moral requirement for energy politics', in D. Mac Lean and P.G. Brown (eds) *Energy and the Future*, Totowa, NJ: Rowman and Littlefield.

Macklin, R. (1981) 'Can future generations correctly be said to have rights?', in E. Partridge (ed.) *Responsibilities to Future Generations*, Buffalo: Prometheus Books.

Meadows, D. (1972) *The Limits to Growth*. New York: Signet Books.

Mitchell, R.K., Agle, B.R. and Wood, D.J. (1997) 'Toward a theory of stakeholder identification and salience', *Academy of Management Review*, 22: 853–86.

OECD (2001) *Environmental Outlook*, Paris: OECD.

Parfit, D. (1987) *Reasons and Persons*, Oxford: Clarendon.

Partridge, E. (1981) 'Introduction', in E. Partridge (ed.) *Responsibilities to Future Generations*, Buffalo: Prometheus Books.

Prahalad, C.K. and Hart, S.L. (2002) 'The fortune at the bottom of the pyramid', *Strategy and Business*, 26(1st q): 54–67.

Raffernsperger, C. (1999) *Uses of the Precautionary Principle in International Treaties and Agreements*, available online at http://www.biotech-info.net/treaties_and_agreements.html.

Rawls, J. (1972) *A Theory of Justice*, Oxford: Oxford University Press.

Richards, D. (1983) Contractarian theory, intergenerational justice and energy policy, in D. MacLean and P.G. Brown (eds) *Energy and the Future*, Totowa: Rowman and Littlefield.

RIVM (1998) *Milieubalans 1998* (in Dutch) [Environmental balance 1998], Alphen aan de Rijn: Samson.

RIVM, (1988) *Concern for Tomorrow: A National Environmental Survey 1985–2010*, Bilthoven: RIVM.

RIVM (1994) *National Environmental Outlook, 1993–2015*, Bilthoven: RIVM.

Roome, N. (ed.) (1998) *Sustainability Strategies for Industry: The Future of Corporate Strategy*, Washington, DC: Island Press.

Roome, N. (2001) 'Conceptualizing and studying the contribution of networks in environmental management and sustainable development', *Business Strategy and the Environment*, 10: 69–76.

Rotmans, J. and De Vries, B. (1997) *Perspectives on Global Change: The Targets Approach*, Cambridge: Cambridge University Press.

Rowley, T.J. (1997) 'Moving beyond dyadic ties: a network theory of stakeholder influences', *The Academy of Management Review*, 22(4): 887–910.

Sen, A. (1999) *Development as Freedom*, New York: Knopf.

Shell International Ltd (1998) *Profits and Principles*, London: Shell.

Sidgwick, H. (1907) *The Methods of Ethics*, 7th edn, New York: Macmillan.

SEC (2001) *De winst van waarden* (in Dutch) [Corporate social responsibility], The Hague: Social Economic Council.

Susskind, L. (1999a) 'Super-optimization: a new approach to national environmental policy-making', paper delivered to the Seminar on Sustainable Development: Towards a New Balance between Environment, Economy, and Social Welfare, The Hague: VROM

Susskind, L. (1999b) *The Consensus Building Handbook*, London: Sage Publications.

Svendsen, A. (1998) *The Stakeholder Strategy*, San Francisco: Berret-Koehler Publishers.

UNCED (1992) *Agenda 21*, New York: United Nations.

UNEP (1997) *Global Environmental Outlook*, New York: Oxford University Press.

Van Luijk, H. (1993) *Om redelijk gewin: Oefening in bedrijfsethiek* (in Dutch) [For a fair profit: Exercises in business ethics], Amsterdam: Boom.

Van Luijk, H. (1994) 'Rights and interests in a participatory market society', *Business Ethics Quarterly*, 4(1): 79–96.

Van Luijk, H. and Schilder, A. (1997) *Patronen van verantwoordelijkheid: Ethiek en corporate governance* (in Dutch) [Patterns of responsibility: Ethics and corporate governance], Amsterdam: Academic Service.

Velasquez, M. (1998) *Business ethics: Concepts and Cases*, 4th edn, Upper Saddle River, NJ: Prentice Hall.

Visser 't Hooft, H. Ph. (1999) *Justice to Future Generations and the Environment*, Dordrecht: Kluwer.

Von Schomberg, R.(1998) *Omstreden biotechnologisch innovatie: Van publiek domein naar langetermijnbeleid* (in Dutch) [Contested bio-technological innovations: From public domain to long term policy], Utrecht: Nederlandse Vereniging voor Bio Ethiek.

Von Weiszacker, E.U. , Lovins A.B. , Lovins L.H. (1997) *Factor Four, Doubling Wealthhalving Resource Use*, London: Earthscan.

VROM (1972) *Urgentie nota milieuhygiene* (in Dutch) [Policy document on the urgency of environmental pollution], The Hague: VROM.

VROM (1984) *Meer dan de som der delen: Eerste nota over de planning van het milieubeleid* (in Dutch) [More than the sum of its parts: first policy document on the planning of environmental policy], The Hague: VROM.

VROM (1985) *Indicative Environmental Multi-year Programs, 1986–1990*, The Hague: VROM.

VROM (1989) *National Environmental Policy Plan: To Choose or to Lose* (NEPP1), The Hague: VROM

VROM (1993a) *National Environmental Policy Plan 2: The Environment, Today's Touchstone* (NEPP2), The Hague: SDU.

VROM (1993b) *Onze aarde als provisiekast* (in Dutch) [An inventory of stocks: Our precious earth], Publicatiereeks milieustrategie nr.1993/6, The Hague: VROM.

VROM (1995) *Van saneren naar beheren: Nadere analyse van het thema verspilling* (in Dutch) [From sanitation policies to resource stocks management], The Hague: VROM.

VROM (1997) *Policy Document on Environment and Economy*, The Hague: VROM.

VROM (1998a) *National Environmental Policy Plan 3* (NEPP3), The Hague: VROM.

VROM (1998b) *The Silent Revolution*, The Hague: VROM.

VROM (1999) *Sleutels voor duurzaamheid* (in Dutch) [Keys of sustainability], The Hague: VROM.

VROM (2001a) *National Environmental Policy Plan 4: Where There is a Will, There is a World* (NEPP4), The Hague: VROM.

VROM (2001b) *Op weg naar duurzaam ondernemen* (in Dutch) [On the way to the sustainable enterprise], The Hague: VROM.

Waddock, S. (2002) *Leading Corporate Citizens: Vision, Values, Value Added*, New York: McGraw-Hill.

WBCSD (2002) *Stakeholder Dialogue: The WBCSD's Approach to Engagement*, Geneva: WBCSD.

WCED (1987), *Our Common Future (The Brundtland Report)*, New York: Oxford University Press.

Welford, R. (ed.) (1998) *Corporate Environmental Management*, London: Earthscan.

Wenz, P.S. (1983) 'Ethics, energy policy, and future generations', *Environmental Ethics*, 5: 195–209.

Wenz, P.S. (2001) *Environmental Ethics Today*, Oxford: Oxford University Press.

Weterings, R., Kuyper, J. and Smeets, E. (1997) *81 Options: Technology for Sustainable Development*, The Hague: VROM.

Wheeler, D. and Sillanpaa, M. (1997) *The Stakeholder Corporation*, London: Pitman Publishing.

Wilson, E.O. (2001) *The Diversity of Life*, Middlesex: Penguin.

Wilson, E.O. (2002) *The Future of Life*, New York: Alfred A. Knopf.

WRR (Netherlands Scientific Council for Government Policy) (1995) *Sustained Risks: A Lasting Phenomenon*, Reports to the Government, no.44, The Hague: SDU.

WSSD (United Nations 'World Summit on Sustainable Development') (2002) *The Johannesburg Declaration on Sustainable Development*, draft political declaration, advanced unedited version of 4 September 2002 (A/conf.199/L.6/rev.2), New York: United Nations.

Index

Printed in the United States
by Baker & Taylor Publisher Services